THOMAS KEITH MEIER

Defoe and the Defense of Commerce

English Literary Studies
University of Victoria
1987

ENGLISH LITERARY STUDIES
Published at the University of Victoria

FOUNDER AND GENERAL EDITOR
Samuel L. Macey

EDITORIAL BOARD
Thomas R. Cleary
Patricia J. Köster
Victor A. Neufeldt
Reginald C. Terry

ADVISORY EDITORS
David Fowler, *University of Washington*
William Frost, *University of California, Santa Barbara*
Donald Greene, *University of Southern California*
Juliet McMaster, *University of Alberta*
Richard J. Schoeck, *University of Colorado*

BUSINESS MANAGER
Hedy Miller

ISBN 0-920604-29-3

The ELS Monograph Series is published in consultation with members of the Department by ENGLISH LITERARY STUDIES, Department of English, University of Victoria, B.C., Canada.

ELS Monograph Series No. 38
© 1987 by Thomas Keith Meier

for Mila

CONTENTS

INTRODUCTION	The Literary Environment of Commerce	7
CHAPTER I	Defoe's Economic Environment	17
CHAPTER II	Defoe's Praise of Commerce	36
CHAPTER III	Defoe's *Tour* as a Paean of Business	56
CHAPTER IV	Defoe's Business Ethics	79
CHAPTER V	Defoe's Reputation	97
	Note on the Texts	109
	Notes	109

INTRODUCTION

THE LITERARY ENVIRONMENT OF COMMERCE

Today the need for a defense of commerce is self-evident. Corporations have long-established public relations departments as a protective measure, and any newspaper reader is no doubt familiar with the more common causes of commercial discomfort. These include the usual risks associated with running a business in an uncertain economic environment while attempting to satisfy the sometimes conflicting demands of customers, employees, and stockholders while at the same time attempting to meet external threats from various agencies of foreign and domestic governments or from the occasional hostile bursts of public opinion. In the United States, problems of business typically concern possible new taxes upon an industry, Justice Department suits blocking a merger, Securities and Exchange Commission orders prohibiting the trading of a particular stock, or Congressional inquiries into the pricing or quality-control practices of a group of companies. In England and France, the issue is often the nationalization or privatization of an industry; elsewhere, news of the expropriation of a foreign (usually American) company and rumors that nations may repudiate their debts are almost routine. Besides these active threats to commercial survival there exist innumerable literary challenges, ranging from best-selling attacks upon industrial safety, pollution, and organizational life to Marxist denunciations with a more specialized appeal. Business is often regarded as an embodiment of a far-from-perfect status quo, and as such it is a prime target for any proponent of social change.

This was not always the case. In seventeenth- and eighteenth-century England, commerce represented the force of social innovation and was supported by radical thinkers. In Daniel Defoe's lifetime, the problem of defending commerce was thus fundamentally different from that faced by its defenders today. Instead of painstakingly demonstrating that commercial practices foster rather than inhibit social progress, Defoe was at pains to show that commerce enhanced rather than destroyed the best features of the older aristocratic order. While lauding the advantages of upward social mobility which are still stressed by Defoe's followers today, he also had to maintain the suitability of commercial employment for the sons of the nobility. Rather than defending commerce from those who sought to replace it, Defoe attempted to calm the fears of those who saw commerce threatening to replace their own way of life.

Any investigator of Defoe's economic thought has the benefit of the important works of J. R. Moore, Maximillian Novak, and Michael Shinagel.[1] There is at present little to add to their discussions of economic matters revealed in Defoe's fiction. The present study, therefore, is concerned solely with the matter of Defoe's opinions toward business — its function, its potential, and its place in the scheme of things — as revealed in his major non-fictional economic writings. This study is not intended, then, as an encyclopedic survey of Defoe's commercial thought nor as another chapter in the continuing debates on whether Defoe was a mercantilist or a free trader or whether Crusoe's island is a theoretical model of a capitalistic or a communistic economy.

DEFINING THE TERMS OF COMMERCE

Because much of the nomenclature associated with business has undergone some change since the eighteenth century, the definition of terms deserves some attention. To signify commercial activity I shall use various terms such as *business* and *trade* in their modern sense. *Business* is the over-arching term which includes all the branches of activity carried on in an enterprise organized for profit. Thus present-day graduate schools of *business* offer courses in marketing, finance, production (sometimes termed "manufacturing"), transportation (often considered an integral part of marketing), and "agribusiness," which involves the planning, financing, preparation, and in some cases the manufacture of agricultural goods for their markets. In the case of many foodstuffs, the processing necessary may be slight, but other commodities such as wool or timber require considerable manufacture before they reach their ultimate consumers. England in Defoe's lifetime was on the threshold of the Industrial Revolution, and its economy, like that of any other pre-industrial nation, was based largely on agricultural commodities.

Business, then, includes the main branches of gainful enterprise — industry, commerce, and the commercial and industrial, or "agribusiness" content of agriculture. *Industry* denotes mining and manufacturing operations. *Commerce* connotes chiefly the activities of buying and selling goods and services, although in Defoe's time as in our own the term in certain contexts has included the financial function, that is, the buying and selling of money. Thus we speak of the Commercial Revolution, which is generally assumed to have run its course by 1700, and which involved the establishment not only of large-scale international trade but also of a highly sophisticated system of credit to support it. *Trade* is a slightly less prestigious term than commerce, and it lacks its financial connotation.

In discussing those who conduct industrial and commercial affairs, I shall need to use the term *businessman* (in Defoe's day, business was almost always conducted by men) — a term which, like *business*, was rarely used in the eighteenth century — to describe those who direct mining, manufacturing, banking, and brokering enterprises along with professional buyers and sellers, whether large or small, foreign or domestic, wholesale or retail. In the eighteenth century, those named *merchants* were usually considered persons of stature, either because of the size of their operations or because they dealt in wholesale goods or foreign commerce, two of the activities which conferred status in the mercantile community. *Tradesman*, on the other hand, often signified a smaller operator. Many tradesmen were, of course, artisans as well as retail salesmen, and their number included such familiar types as shoemakers, blacksmiths, and tailors. A *shopkeeper* was definitely a small-scale retailer.

Another prefatory matter which should be mentioned is the approach to Defoe's spelling and punctuation. The best scholarly editions available at present reproduce Defoe's texts in various ways, including facsimile, transcription of manuscript, and modernized spelling and capitalization. For the sake of consistency I have chosen to modernize Defoe's spelling and capitalization but to avoid tampering with his punctuation (including italics) because of the danger of distorting his meaning.

BUSINESS AS AN INTELLECTUAL MOVEMENT

Defoe's role as a defender of commerce has never been seriously doubted. If anything, he has been granted prominence and even uniqueness as an economic writer of his time far too easily and unquestioningly. He is often mentioned as "the finest journalist — or at any rate industrial correspondent — of his time,"[2] "the first great apologist of the English middle class,"[3] or "the complacent apologist of nascent industrial capitalism."[4] One of our best literary histories states that "one of Defoe's chief merits is his firm grasp of social and economic problems, based on sound and careful observation. Here he rose superior to the polite Augustans who despised him."[5] However significant we may choose to think Defoe in the field of economic journalism and however important we may decide to pronounce him in the realm of capitalist apologetics — and he was indeed the dominant figure of his age — if we are to understand his place in the relationship between business and literature, we must take care not to exalt him to the exclusion of other writers. We do Defoe's reputation a false service by assuming him to be the master of a field which was neglected by the other capable thinkers of his day.

By the eighteenth century, the practice of business and the concerns of literature in England had begun to intersect at an increasing rate. With the growing importance of commerce, increasing numbers of literary figures inevitably came into closer contact with it. Often the contact grew out of the author's own or a father's livelihood being linked to trade, although others became familiar with commerce through Parliamentary debates and royal commissions or through the many controversies on trade which raged in the pamphlets and newspapers of the day. The rapid growth of readership was making substantial merchants of booksellers and, to some extent, making entrepreneurs of writers. But after all is said about the economic backgrounds of writers, about the history of publishing, and about authors' involvement in the politics of trade, to a student of literature the most important index of the relationship between literature and business must remain the way business is reflected in the texts of literary works, and in this period that reflection is substantial.

The Restoration and eighteenth-century works which reflect an awareness of business are extremely varied in genre and authorship and are so numerous as to limit the present remarks to a suggestive rather than a comprehensive summary of them. The quality represented ranges from the splendor of Pope to the obscurity of Yalden and includes such literary types as the periodical essay, the descriptive poem, the drama, the novel, and intellectual prose. The popularity of the eighteenth-century "georgic" — a blank-verse descriptive poem concerned largely with explaining how to do something — testifies to a certain fascination among contemporary poets with the actual techniques of industry and trade. Grainger's *Sugar-Cane*, Dyer's *The Fleece*, Jago's *Edge-Hill*, and Dodsley's *Agriculture* concern themselves largely with industrial processes, but they, like John Gay's *Wine*, also celebrate the function of the merchant in vending the wares produced. Authors as varied as Evelyn,

Denham, Addison, Pope, Young, Savage, Blackmore, Glover, and Thomson make use of a wide range of genres to emphasize the benefits of trade and industry to England and to civilization generally. In forms as varied as an essay by Steele, a drama by Lillo, and a novel by Brooke, we find emphasis upon the educational value of participating in commerce and the dignity of the position of the merchant in society.

A survey of the opinions about business expressed by Restoration and eighteenth-century writers would reveal that a great many authors other than Defoe were interested in the current operations and the future promise of commerce and industry. Many were favorably inclined toward business, seeing it as a great civilizing force and as a means of attaining both widespread material prosperity and world peace, two of the perennial dreams of mankind. These conclusions are readily apparent from a reading of contemporary works which touch on commerce, but they are conclusions for which a twentieth-century reader is somewhat unprepared. Our better literary, political, and economic histories take ample note of the fact that the eighteenth and late seventeenth centuries are a period of increasing business activity, of social change due to the rise of a middle-class supported by earnings from business, of rapidly-improving transportation and rapidly-expanding trade. It is, as we well know, the period which was the culmination of the Commercial and the beginning of the Industrial Revolutions. Much has indeed been written about the growth of a middle-class readership and its influence on the increasing popularity of prose, particularly upon the rise of the newspaper and the novel.[6]

Despite this background, we may be unprepared to encounter a climate of intellectual acceptance of the aims and promise of commerce not only in the newspapers, novels, and plays that catered to mass audiences but also in the verse and intellectual prose of the period. Doubtless the tendency to overlook this widespread literary enthusiasm for business is largely due to twentieth-century literary conditioning. The characters in popular modern novels about business—*Babbitt*, *Cash McCall*, *The Man in the Gray Flannel Suit*, *A World of Profit*, or *Sincerely Willis Wayde*—are usually unscrupulous and unattractive corporate wheeler-dealers or downtrodden, faceless corporate servants. The conditioning provided by this body of literature and by the culture which produced it continually manifests itself in our thinking and is largely responsible for such critical assessments as Bonamy Dobree's rejection of the honesty of Fenton, Glover, Tickell, Young, and Dyer: "It must be confessed that much of this [their praise of commerce] does not ring quite true; it all smacks too much of mercantilism, too much of the colonial expansion policy favoured by Chatham; we feel that many of the pious vaunts are, if not deliberate self-deception, at least what we should call wishful thinking."[7] There is absolutely no warrant in the text of these authors' works for such an assertion, nor has it been proved that mercantilists and expansionists were less honest than other ideologists. In fact, the most prominent characteristic of most of the poems to which Dobree refers is a wholehearted endorsement of commerce. They constitute a fervent litany of the blessings of trade and are indeed so repetitive of each other as to bespeak perhaps more conviction than art.

Criticism of Thomson's poetry quite plainly illustrates the matter of twentieth-century subjectivity. R. D. Havens points out that Thomson is quite capable of simultaneously cherishing notions of commercial progress and cultural primitivism. This is indeed a just observation, but Havens and Patricia Meyer Spacks would have us believe that Thomson tends to favor primitivism, and they both maintain that Thomson actually wrote better poetry when discussing primitivism and simple nature than when he was extolling the virtues of commerce.[8] Perhaps in the twentieth century we merely assume primitive topics to be a subject more fit for poetry than we do commercial ones. (The eighteenth century, to be sure, is often denominated as a period which insisted upon rigid standards for determining the fitness of particular subjects for poetic treatment, but the Augustans themselves apparently found commerce a sufficiently poetic theme.) It was of course within the talents of the author of *Sophonisba* to write bad lines on most of the subjects he described, but he could make good verses on many of them as well; his statement of the goal of the British merchant,

> Round social earth to circle fair exchange
> And bind the nations in a golden chain,

is a sound poetic expression when viewed technically and a splendid conception when considered abstractly, but to generations for whom Sinclair Lewis has been required reading, it inevitably (and unfortunately, for the sake of our own objectivity) summons up echoes of Rotarian luncheon oratory.[9]

To be sure, there was a gradual lessening of literary enthusiasm for commerce toward the end of the eighteenth century. Johnson's balanced moral strictures and the pessimism of Goldsmith, Cowper, and Blake occur late in the century, presaging the condemnations of Crabbe and Wordsworth. George Sherburn believes this change in attitude to be one of the "long-term chastening effects" of the bursting of the South Sea bubble, which caused "a revulsion from the mercantilist worship of commerce to the physiocratic idea that wealth comes basically from the soil."[10] There is a noticeable physiocratic sympathy in many of these later authors' works, but if the fall of South Sea stock in 1720 was its primary cause, then it was indeed a long-term effect. The commercial raptures of Thomson, Lillo, Brooke, and Young all followed the crash of 1720, as did the economic theorizing of Burke, Hume, and Adam Smith. The revulsion against commerce in the eighteenth century was tentative and scattered; it did not constitute a "movement" in that it was neither particularly widespread nor sufficiently explicit in defining the basis of its opposition. Certainly this opposition was at least partially based on physiocratism, for evidence of it is embedded in many of their works, notably those of Cowper and Goldsmith. A certain portion of this opposition seems to have grown out of the traditional classical praise of the virtues of the countryside and the perennial moral condemnation of the vices of avarice and luxury. The basis for opposition also may have been part of a natural reaction to question or doubt the extravagant claims made for commerce by its zealous proponents.

There has been a natural tendency to think of these proponents as Whigs and their adversaries as Tories, but commerce was in reality a national cause which crossed party lines. Addison and Steele, Ambrose Phillips, Thomas Tickell, and Thomson (whom McKillop labels a "Whig panegyrist of progress"[11]) all fit into the stereotyped categorization. Pope, Swift, and Prior, on the other hand, are usually considered to be Tories, yet they wrote approvingly of commerce. True, they had been Whigs early in their careers, but the fact that they did change parties without altering their opinions of commerce is in itself significant. Swift's *Drapier's Letters*, which are pro-commerce insofar as they portray a decent and intelligent tradesman-persona, came out after his conversion to Toryism and actually were written in opposition to Walpole's Whig regime. Burke later maintained that the poetry of Pope, Glover, and Johnson was a contributing cause to England's engagement in the War of the Austrian Succession, a war fought to protect British commercial interests.[12] The well-publicized changes of party affiliation among eighteenth-century writers illustrate that while there existed identifiably different ideologies between the two parties, the Tories tending toward landed and high-church interests and the Whigs leaning toward commercial and Dissenting concerns, there was no sharp demarcation between them. Thus writers could change parties with little fear of stigma, and the political leaders of the City could vigorously attack such important props of Walpole's Whig hegemony as rotten boroughs and the Septennial Act.

Wilkes himself, after arousing a succession of middle-class mobs to his cause, became a Tory in his later years. Despite this turn of events, however, George Rude demonstrates that business was at the center of the radical movements for political reform and for greater civil liberties.[13] The City councils, the City M.P.s, and the Lord Mayor, often backed by mobs of tradesmen, craftsmen, or urban wage-earners, developed gradually into a force for progressive reform. Yet this process was not obvious to many contemporary observers. Charles Churchill, Wilkes' ardent supporter, frequently vented his rage upon Wilkes' City followers, as in his mention of "The cit, a Common-Councilman by place, / Ten thousand mighty nothings in his face."[14] James Beattie evidently assumed that Churchill's poetic following was among these same citizens Churchill delighted in castigating, for he too attacks them in his derisive verses on Churchill: "...though thousand cits admire thy rage, / Though less of fool than felon marks thy page...."[15] Confusions such as these among contemporary observers serve to demonstrate the complexity of political alignments in the period.

Defoe's political career, like those of Prior and Pope, is also an illustrative one. His practice of writing for both Whig and Tory journals is well known, but the fact that he commented rapturously upon commerce in journals of both persuasions is rarely noticed. His *Review*, which contains much lavish praise of business, was written at Harley's instigation to support the Tories. The value of commerce was thus not really a matter for partisan debate in the eighteenth century. As C. A. Moore declares, "commercial prosperity had come to be almost the universal and unchallenged concern of the nation [after 1714]... The essential question was, not whether trade should be given all possible encouragement, but what were the wisest measures for the purpose."[16] Commerce and industry had caught the literary imagination of the period and represented, for a time at least, the progressive hope of the future. Through business, humankind might gain better control over the environment, might raise the general standard of living, might even prevent war. Conceived in these terms, commerce exerted a great appeal not only for the person of practical affairs but for the poet and intellectual as well. On Defoe, a man of both practical and literary susceptibilities, it exerted an irresistible influence, and he indeed became the chief apostle of business in his time. Had there been no such climate of intellectual acceptance of commerce and industry among his literary peers, however, one may doubt that he would have written so copiously on his subject or have found an audience for his work.

While praise of business and businessmen came from members of both parties, such praise was less than universal, and authors who seem generally favorable to tradesmen were not always so. Yet those who sneered at trade, like those who praised it, were divided between the two parties. Thus a Tory such as Swift could deride Whigs, who "came with the spirit of *shop-keepers* to frame rules for the administration of kingdom; or, as if they thought the whole art of government consisted in the importation of nutmegs, and the curing of herring."[17] A Whig such as Burke could make the same point: "Society is, indeed, a contract. Subordinate contracts for objects of mere occasional interest may be dissolved at pleasure, but the state ought not to be considered as nothing better than a partnership in a trade of pepper and coffee, calico or tobacco, or some other low concern...."[18] It is interesting to note that while such detractions carry an aristocratic tone, there is very little evidence of any particular bias against trade by British aristocrats themselves. Chesterfield takes a uniformly favorable view of commerce in his letters to his son, frequently making such comments as, "Since you turn your thoughts a little towards trade and commerce, which I am very glad you do...."[19] British noblemen not only sought to repair their fortunes by marrying City heiresses but also attempted to improve their patrimonies through both commercial investments and entrepreneurial ventures. After marshalling an impressive list of these noble entrepreneurs, Diana Spearman concludes that "trade was not a class preserve but an interest of the whole nation."[20]

Although commerce had its detractors in the Restoration and eighteenth century, they were far outnumbered by its enthusiasts. Business was, in fact, one of the few public causes in Britain which united most of the varied interests of the period. It held appeal for aristocrat and commoner, layman and cleric, intellectual and man of affairs, Whig and Tory, artist and citizen. Defoe's interest in commerce, therefore, should not be considered unique. He may have written a great deal more on commerce and occasionally he may have written with greater insight than did his contemporaries, but his was no lone voice in the wilderness. Defoe's writings on commerce should be examined not as the effusions of a solitary apostle of the middle class but as his particular contribution to a generally-accepted national cause.

CHAPTER I

Defoe's Economic Environment

Daniel Defoe was actively involved in the economic affairs of his day both as a businessman and a journalist; he was intensely aware of the commercial conditions and controversies of his period. Indeed, one of the best methods for us to become acquainted with those conditions and controversies is to read his works, a method used by many economic historians and attested to by the multitude of references to Defoe's writings which crowd their footnotes. Before entering upon a detailed examination of Defoe's works, however, it would be well to outline briefly the state of the economic environment in which he worked, the intellectual climate in which he reasoned, and the social milieu in which he aspired.

BUSINESS CONDITIONS IN DEFOE'S DAY

Defoe lived during the beginnings of the modern economic era. The Commercial Revolution, usually considered to have covered the period 1500-1750, was virtually complete by his death. The Agricultural Revolution, generally placed around 1688-1793, had begun during his young manhood. Although the Industrial Revolution, often considered to have been underway by 1750, largely postdated him, he and other contemporary observers did take an interest in such industrial enterprises as were already in operation during the first quarter of the eighteenth century; at the turn of the century Defoe was himself a brick and tile manufacturer employing a hundred workmen.[1] Defoe was well-placed chronologically to become a spokesman for commerce and industry because most of the significant elements necessary to the practice of modern business were already present, even if in rudimentary form, during his lifetime.

Of these various revolutions, the Commercial is most important for our purposes, not only because it has more relevance to the life and thought of Defoe than do the others but also because it developed the markets, provided the capital, and supplied the techniques of financing necessary for the Agricultural and Industrial Revolutions.[2] The chief components of the Commercial Revolution were the growth of foreign trade and the development of a sizable capital market. To be sure, domestic trade was growing, and Defoe gives us a comprehensive view of it in his *Tour*, but its increase was hampered by the sorry state of internal transportation in England. The road system, physically poor and infested with highwaymen, was used for pack trains, postal services, and driving cattle, sheep, and geese to market. Coastal shipping and inland waterways provided the chief means of internal transport; the great advances in canals and turnpikes came after the mid-eighteenth century, but some work was being done on deepening and straightening existing waterways during the first half of the eighteenth century.

Exports grew from £2.5 million in 1613 to £6.5 million in 1700, with most of the gain accomplished during the last forty years of the period; imports rose from £2 million to £6 million. Woolen cloth was, of course, the chief export of the period, but while it had made up around 90 percent of exports in 1621, it constituted only some 50 percent in 1700. Although the wool trade continued to increase, much of the growth in exports was in coal, tin, lead, and also wheat in years when the crop was good. Re-export of cotton goods, spices, and drugs from the Orient was also on the rise. Imports consisted largely of iron, grain, and naval stores from the Baltic, wines from France and Portugal, tobacco, timber, and sugar from America, the West Indies, and the Levant. It also should not be forgotten that much of the English trade with the American and West Indian colonies consisted of traffic in slaves from Africa.

Trade and shipping during the seventeenth century differ in three marked respects from that carried on today. In the first place, because communication was no faster than transportation, the master of a merchant vessel was a great deal more important then than now. While many ships plied a routine trade between regularly-scheduled ports, most did not. A ship's captain might well find that the market for his cargo had drastically softened at its originally-scheduled port or that the supply of the commodity he had planned to take on there was non-existent or its price prohibitive. In such cases he had to use his own judgment and usually was empowered to seek out opportunities at other ports and even to sell the ship if a favorable opportunity beckoned. Once away from his home port the master was largely on his own.

Another difference between seventeenth-century and present-day shipping is that much of the seventeenth-century trade was illegal. During the course of the century, however, the trade monopolies were slowly abandoned or abolished, and by 1700 most English trade was taxed rather than prohibited. A final important difference between trade conditions then and now is that other than import and export duties and excises, all of which are taxes upon the consumers rather than the sellers of goods (although they may affect demand), the merchant paid no direct taxes to the Crown. Besides customs duties, the other major source of government revenue was taxes upon real estate, which fell heaviest upon the landed interest and which continued in the form of taxes upon chimneys or windows even after the modern ad valorum tax upon real estate was introduced. By 1715, the land taxed amounted to less than 20 percent of the royal revenues of £5.5 million, and excises and customs accounted for over 70 percent. When we recall this fact, Johnson's definition of the traditionally unpopular excise as "a hateful tax levied upon commodities" becomes more meaningful to twentieth-century readers.

The development of a system of modern finance in England was another product of the Commercial Revolution. Such a system had existed in several important Italian and Belgian centers during the Middle Ages, of course, and Amsterdam had emerged as a major money market in the sixteenth century. Large-scale trading ventures such as the East India, Levant, Turkey, Muscovy, Royal Africa, or Hudson's Bay Companies required considerable capital outlays. While most corporations throughout the eighteenth century continued to be regulated companies, the joint-stock form of ownership developed rapidly. The East India Company began by selling shares in its ships and cargoes for each voyage and by 1657 had begun issuing general shares in all the company's operations. It paid dividends upon these shares, which were traded openly in London. The liability of shareholders in chartered companies was limited to the value of their shares, while investors in unchartered ventures assumed full liability. The joint-stock and limited-liability concepts were of great value in freeing capital for large undertakings, although the bursting of the South Sea Bubble in 1720 served to frighten investors for several generations thereafter; one of the repercussions of this speculative collapse was probably to delay the formal acceptance of the limited-liability concept until the passage of the Corporation Acts of the nineteenth century. Defoe was himself duly impressed by this catastrophe and endlessly counselled caution in dealing with stock-jobbers; in fact, he had been suspicious of equities for some time before the actual crash.

The South Sea Company was founded in 1711 for trade in the Pacific. It took on £9.5 million of the national debt at 5 percent and was granted the Assiento won by the Crown in the Treaty of Utrecht. Although difficulties with the Spanish government ensued, investors in England were so intrigued at the prospect of getting rich in the slave trade that they began to bid up the price of South Sea shares. Several unchartered and under-capitalized companies began to take advantage of the speculative fever by buying South Sea stock; a number of their investors bought shares with money borrowed against South Sea shares. After the South Sea Company brought suit against a number of these companies, they and their owners began wildly attempting to sell their South Sea stock, and shares fell from £1000 to £175, ruining hundreds of overextended investors.[3]

While the South Sea panic ruined many investors and scared many more, it also enhanced the reputation of the Bank of England, which had been founded as a joint-stock company in 1694 and which came through the crisis unscathed. Banking may be said to have begun in England in 1625 with the repeal of the usury laws and the establishment of an 8 percent legal maximum rate of interest. Actually, tradesmen who found themselves in a favorable cash position, particularly scriveners and goldsmiths, had been making loans at interest throughout the sixteenth century. Goldsmiths were particularly well-suited for this function in that they had large strong-boxes designed for the physical protection of valuables. They began by making a modest charge for protecting the coin of their clients and eventually, under pressure of competition, began to offer interest on these deposits. They had established the amount of cash reserve they needed to meet daily calls and loaned the rest at interest. Merchant-depositors began issuing checks in the form of instructions to their goldsmiths to pay certain sums to the bearer on demand. Charles I unwittingly increased the use of goldsmith-bankers in 1641 when he confiscated the gold that had been deposited in the Tower for safekeeping by a sizable number of merchants. The mercantile community thereafter preferred to entrust their deposits to goldsmiths or other tradesmen rather than to the Crown. By 1650, goldsmiths were issuing their own notes which circulated as money. During the second half of the seventeenth century, normal business transactions came to be generally carried out without the actual transfer of coin from hand to hand. The establishment of the Bank of England in 1694, then, was in important event but not a radical innovation in the financial life of England.

The history of commerce is largely a history of devices developed to minimize risk. Chartered, limited-liability companies, modern banking services, and insurance were techniques for limiting risk developed by the businessmen of the seventeenth century. By the end of the century there were a number of companies organized to write life, fire, and marine insurance. The modern system of commerce had been established.

The Agricultural Revolution was hardly in evidence by Defoe's death in 1731. Townshend did not begin his agricultural improvements until he left office in 1730; Jethro Tull's *The New Horse Hoeing Husbandry* did not appear until 1733, and Bakewell's experiments with sheep-breeding were a generation in the future. Arthur Young, the great propagandist of improved agricultural techniques, whose career resembled Defoe's in that he was as great a failure at farming as Defoe was in business, was not born until 1741. Nevertheless, some experimentation had been undertaken, such as Weston's use of turnips and clover as feed for cattle, and the Royal Society's interest in proper preparation of the soil; furthermore, agricultural production in the first quarter of the eighteenth century was sufficient to support the relatively stable population, the wool trade, and occasional exports of wheat. After 1688, the enclosure movement gained some momentum through the piecemeal authorization of enclosure by Private Acts of Parliament.

Industry during Defoe's lifetime was conducted largely on the domestic system, and mostly without the use of external power, but those generalizations hold only because of the predominance of the wool industry in England. Other operations such as coal and tin mining, printing, brewing, sugar-refining, and pottery-, glass-, and brick-making had become organized on a factory basis. In addition, water power was already being applied in the silk and iron industries. Certain industries such as pinmaking took advantage of the principle of division of labor, with several craftsmen performing different tasks in the same shop. The cotton industry, a relatively new one in the seventeenth century, was organized from its beginnings on a capitalistic basis, with an owner providing both raw materials and tools to large numbers of workers under one roof. Even in the wool manufacture of the West of England similar practices existed, often with over a hundred workmen in one establishment. By Defoe's death all that remained to produce the modern factory system was the application of power machinery.

Because Defoe made such a frequent point of the superiority of English commerce and manufacturing over those of the rest of Europe, it would be well briefly to examine these matters. Both Gregory King in 1695 and Adam Smith in 1775 put Holland first and England *second*, on a per capita annual income basis. On a national income basis, King again placed England second, this time to France.[4] As to manufactures, "it was probably not until after the introduction of the spinning jenny, the steam engine, and Cort's puddling process that English industry became absolutely larger as well as relatively more efficient than its French counterpart."[5]

In this case, Defoe assumed British manufacturing to be superior because of the well-attested fact of active French recruitment of skilled English labor. This, he reasoned, was evidence of French inferiority, whereas in fact it was somewhat analogous to the problem of the "brain drain" Britain faces today and indicated better opportunity abroad. At times Defoe may have exaggerated England's commercial importance to make a polemical point, but with the scarcity of contemporary statistical records, it was difficult for observers at the time — as it has been for later historians — to make accurate analyses of seventeenth- and eighteenth-century conditions.

CONTEMPORARY ECONOMIC THEORY

The prevailing economic thought of Defoe's era has been dubbed "mercantilism" by later observers, but it is a difficult set of beliefs to understand without at least a cursory glance at the theoretical system which preceded it. The dominant economic theory of the Middle Ages, canonism, grew out of contemporary speculations on Christian ethics and was ultimately codified into Canon law. The guiding principle of canonism is the condemnation of all economic activity beyond that necessary to support an individual in a hereditary station in life. To do more was to be guilty of avarice, one of the seven deadly sins. So deeply rooted in Western culture was this concept that long after the demise of canonism as a viable economic theory, there was a strong tendency to identify economic aspiration with avarice, as may readily be seen by a review of seventeenth- and eighteenth-century imaginative literature.[6]

The most significant aspect of canonism is its refusal to consider capital as a factor of production. At the local level there was a very small requirement for capital goods beyond the artisan's hand tools, and there was scant need for monetary exchange since barter appears to have been significant. This attitude toward capital resulted in two of the most important features of canonist thought, the prohibition of usury and the doctrine of just price. With so little use for capital, the only need for borrowing would occur in times of emergency, at which times the Church taught that Christian charity, not the desire to take advantage of a neighbor's adversity, should apply. Thus to charge rent for so sterile a thing as money (which was not recognized to have a time value) was both avaricious and uncharitable.

Just price, a formulation from Aristotle via Aquinas, was a device used to maintain a stable society. The ideal in exchanges of goods was for the farmer or artisan to receive payment for agricultural or manufactured goods exactly equal to the expenses and labor used to produce the article; otherwise it was thought that either the buyer or the seller must necessarily incur a monetary loss. Since cost accounting from earliest times has been reckoned a problematical art, Aquinas makes the governors of the state responsible for establishing the just price, but in actual practice the clergy and the guild masters cooperated in setting prices. In most cases the price set was the "vulgar" or market price, but the public authorities became involved chiefly in times of scarcity, to prevent sellers from charging inordinately high prices.

These were the broad outlines of canonist doctrine. The new attitudes and new discoveries of the Renaissance spelled the doom of canonism, and the expansion of foreign trade rendered its tenets unworkable. It should be remembered, however, that throughout the Middle Ages there was a lively foreign trade in luxuries for the upper classes and that kings and nobles often had recourse to usurers to outfit their armies for imminent campaigns. The precepts of canonism and the forces of a purely local economy generally applied only to the artisans, small tenants, and laborers who made up the bulk of the Medieval population; the nobility participated in a more complex and cosmopolitan set of economic relationships.

With the geographical discoveries and increased trade of the Renaissance this economic complexity became widely diffused through European society and eventually rendered the doctrine of canonism obsolete. The theory which replaced it has come to be called mercantilism, which is not a school of economic thought in the modern sense but rather a loosely-related body of writings which expressed contemporary economic opinions from the Renaissance until the end of the eighteenth century. Perhaps the most important political fact of this period was the development of nation-states, and mercantilism is often regarded as the economic rationalization of nationalism and the ideological prop of absolute monarchy. The doctrines of mercantilism are indeed nationalistic to their core, and in England seventeenth-century Parliamentarians and eighteenth-century Whigs were among the staunchest mercanilists. It was Cromwell, after all, who instituted the important Navigation Acts, which are solidly mercantilistic in purpose. Far from exalting absolute monarchy or divine right, many mercantilists in England linked the cause of liberty to that of mercantile expansion. Thus Henry Robinson, writing in 1649, argues: "If then we desire to be long free from the yoke of foreign dominion, and to enjoy that liberty, which we have so dearly purchased, it concerns us seriously, to inquire into all the ways and means, whereby trade and navigation may be increased unto the utmost."[7]

Robinson's statement provides an insight into the guiding motive behind mercantilism — the quest for national security and self-sufficiency. Briefly defined, then, mercantilism is a loosely-coordinated body of beliefs which held that the national interest was best served by the encouragement of that foreign commerce which produced a favorable balance of trade. The mercantilists emphasized foreign trade above all other forms of economic activity, just as the eighteenth-century Physiocrats were later to stress agriculture and as many nineteenth-century theorists were to dwell upon industry. International trade was deemed the only source of wealth in a country without gold or silver mines, and this basic assertion is repeated endlessly in bullionist literature. In order to capture foreign bullion, England enacted numerous laws and duties aimed at increasing the value of exports above that of imports, thus resulting in a net inflow of specie. In most writers this goal of attracting precious metals from abroad is presented in a sophisticated fashion, making the national objective one of increasing the national stock of money on an aggregate basis rather than being overly concerned with attaining a favorable balance on each individual transaction.

The notion of the importance of a favorable trade balance, however, rests upon two basic assumptions which have often been regarded as faulty by later economists. The first assumption is that of the two parties to a particular transaction, one must emerge a winner and the other a loser. In much mercantilistic writing, trade is assumed to be a form of pecuniary warfare in which whatever is gained by one party is considered as lost by the other. The mercantilist era was on the wane before this belief was supplanted on a wide scale by the idea that in most transactions both parties tend to gain and that this fact is responsible for inducing them to strike the bargain in the first place. The second questionable assumption concerns the mercantilist confusion of money with capital. Adam Smith came down very hard upon this point in the eighteenth century, as has Jacob Viner in the twentieth.[8] While there is some controversy as to the exact extent of the mercantilist identification case for this belief. He also insists that Defoe's proposals for a national program of forced saving, for nationalization of the merchant marine with a provision for half-pay for idle seamen, and other such social projects "were in no way farsighted, prophetic predictions of modern social security and unemployment insurance, for they looked back rather than forward."[12] This is a rather silly matter for Novak to get tangled in, because the question of whether these measures are forward- or backward-looking is in the long run a moot one. The terms "forward" and "backward" carry implicit value judgments, and their use ignores the fact that many economic ideas crop up recurrently through history. Thus the theory of just price, which is at the heart of canonism, bears a striking resemblance to the labor theory of value, which is central to Marxist economic theory. Defoe and many other projectors of the seventeenth and eighteenth century put forward proposals to deal with unemployment and other social ills. Proposals similar to some of his have been adopted in the twentieth century. This is not to say that he influenced these later events or that he was "farsighted," but it does indicate similarities between some of Defoe's and some modern thought. For that matter, ours is to some extent a neo-mercantilist age; current concern over balances of payments and gold drains is similar to that of the seventeenth-century mercantilists.

BUSINESS AND THE WORK ETHIC

Modern economic attitudes, of course, resemble mercantilist theory more closely than they do the Medieval viewpoint. Two of the chief intellectual forces which served to invigorate mercantilism, and which may also be seen as later affecting the thought of Adam Smith and the classical school, were the idea of progress, largely impelled by Baconian science, and the transformation of Christian attitudes toward business, largely influenced by the development of the Protestant ethic.

By the seventeenth century, mercantilism had established itself as a socially legitimate mode of thought and action. From the questionable Medieval status of a social parasite, the merchant had progressed to the position of being hailed as a defender of the realm and a benefactor of humankind. This shift of attitude is so fundamental and its consequences so important that it has fueled a controversy over its causes that has raged from the beginning of the twentieth century to the present. Despite the controversial nature of the discussion, however, there is general agreement in the belief that the development of Protestant theoretical economics. This is a more difficult task than one might imagine, for Defoe contradicts, in one or another of the pamphlets attributed to him, virtually every economic pronouncement he makes. He usually invokes theory only in order to reinforce particular arguments of topical interest; depending upon which political party or issue he was supporting at the time, he might invoke a theoretical position which he had formerly dismissed as invalid. William Lee saw Defoe as a free trader. After Lee, the major authority on Defoe's economic thought was J. R. Moore, who maintains that "Lee overstated the case for Defoe as a free trader; but he was far nearer the truth than the writers who would represent him as a Whig protectionist...."[10] Moore's treatment of Defoe, however, is more appreciative than analytical and does not deal systematically with his economic thought. Moore's chief interest lies in pointing out the similarity between Defoe's utterances and a position later taken by Cardinal Alberoni or a dissimilarity between Defoe's pronouncement and those of Bishop Hoadley or Bernard Mandeville. Moore stresses, incidentally, the differences between Defoe's and Mandeville's positions on luxurious living, but as we shall see in our discussion of Defoe's business ethics, he shared some common ground with Mandeville.

Maximillian E. Novak has presented perhaps the best elucidation of Defoe's position, which he terms eclectic but firmly based in contemporary mercantilist thought.[11] He demonstrates quite convincingly that Defoe was not primarily a free-trader and thus cannot be thought a progressive in terms of his own era. Defoe seems to have believed implicitly in the favorable balance of trade and in the desirability of gaining bullion, but he was also willing to export raw materials in certain cases. Nor did he advocate keeping wages low. He was unique among contemporary commercial writers in that he felt that the mere circulation of goods within a country enriched it, that as trade became more brisk people's wants expanded, that trade labored harder to meet the new demands and thus employed more hands, and that the nation's stock of wealth was thereby increased. While he deviates profitably from stock mercantilist thought, on occasion at times he neglects some of its more sensible aspects, such as its insistence upon keeping prices low. Moore recognizes most of these deviations from mainstream mercantilist thinking, but he does not make a case for Defoe as a free-trader.

Novak sees Defoe as firmly entrenched in the thought of his predecessors and contemporaries, with occasional theoretical insights, but on the whole a man of his age. For the most part Novak makes an excellent economic thought in the seventeenth century, note this statement by Nicholas Barbon, who is often classed as a mercantilist but is occasionally critical of what tend to be regarded as standard mercantilist policies:

> By *trade*, the natural stock of the country is improved.... The *over-plus* of these wares [cloth, lead, leather, etc.] are transported by the merchants, and exchanged for the wines, oils, spices, and every thing that is good of foreign countries. The trader has one share for his pains, and the landlord the other for his rent: so that by *trade*, the inhabitants in general, are not only well fed, clothed, and lodged, but the richer sort are furnished with all things to promote the ease, pleasure, and pomp of life.[9]

Barbon is in agreement with most mercantilists in his praise of foreign trade and of the favorable balance, but he is somewhat atypical in his emphasis on well-paid labor, his approval of the luxury traffic, and his endorsement of spending rather than investing the monetary surplus.

In mercantilist policy colonies were usually classed as foreign competition rather than as part of the mother commonwealth. The attempt was made to import raw materials from colonies, to add as much value through manufacture as possible, and to reexport the finished goods to the colonies. Acts embodying this policy, of course, eventually contributed to the American Revolution. Chief among other Parliamentary implementations of mercantilist doctrines were tariffs and prohibitions on imported goods (especially upon manufactures and luxuries), protective tariffs for infant industries, the Navigation Acts (which required English goods to be carried in English bottoms), various prohibitions on the export of raw materials (including the death penalty for exporting raw wool), and export bounties on corn, linen and silk goods, beef, and other products of those industries Parliament sought to foster.

Mercantilism, it must be remembered, was not an economic school but a loose congeries of economic opinion and speculation which developed over a lengthy period. Under its influence, however, several important changes took place. It facilitated the transition from the valuation of goods upon an intrinsic or "just-price" basis to one of market value. While it created barriers to foreign trade, it provided an impetus to sweep away a multitude of Medieval duties, tolls, and restrictions that had served to hamper internal trade. Most importantly, perhaps, it formed a part of the mechanism to turn most minds away from the economically static Medieval outlook to a viewpoint which by Defoe's manhood was basically a dynamic one.

Considerable effort has been expended in attempts to discover Defoe's of bullion with wealth, there is at present little doubt that at least some mercantilists were guilty of this confusion and that many of them often wrote as if they were. In extenuation, however, it should be added that in the early mercantilist era, before the formation of large capital markets, specie alone of all tangible assets possessed the liquidity to quickly finance an army or expedition. The English monarchs after Henry VIII, however, lacked a large national treasure and financed their wars by credit or special taxes.

Besides defense, the principal reasons for desiring large balances of money were to serve as an aid to trade and, evidently, to have it for its own sake. While there was no widespread knowledge of the idea that the quantity of money in circulation inversely affects its value, there was the belief that a certain level of money in circulation was needed to "drive" trade; the more money in circulation the faster trade would operate and therefore, given favorable trade balances, the faster money would build up. There was a considerable amount of exhortation of Britons to live thriftily and to avoid consuming luxury goods, toward the end of accumulating money within the national boundaries. This train of thought was congruent with the piety of many seventeenth-century divines, but to the extent that it was successful in creating personal cash reserves, it also created the personal dilemma of deciding how to dispose of such wealth in a non-luxurious, non-avaricious fashion.

After the balance of trade, the most striking feature of mercantilism was its attitude toward employment. Because the aim was to export more valuable goods than were imported, the mercantilists were actually interested in exporting products which had more value added by English labor than the goods they were importing had by foreign labor. This suggested to many mercantilists that in order to secure a favorable trade balance it was imperative to keep English wages low, and that by doing so the country could effectively convert labor into bullion. Thus evolved the mercantilist conviction that people are the riches of a nation. Full employment, low wages, a large population, encouragement of immigration (particularly of foreign craftsmen) and of exports with a high labor content, and discouragement of exports of raw materials were some of the corollaries of the population theory of wealth.

It must be admitted that many of the mercantilists favored keeping wages as close to the subsistence level as possible in the belief that the British wage-earner would work only when driven by necessity. Defoe took frequent exception to this spartan concept of human motivation, as did a number of other mercantilists. As a reminder of the diversity of thought contributed mightily toward the legitimization of business. H. R. Trevor-Roper outlines the nature of the problem in his remark: "But even if we admit the obvious fact that, in some way, Protestantism in the seventeenth century... was the religion of progress, the question remains, in what way?"[13]

Max Weber inaugurated the discussion with his famous essays in which he declared that a new kind of capitalism was established during the Reformation and that Calvinism was the intellectual movement which fostered its growth. Subsequent commentators have challenged his conception of both capitalism and Calvinism, but the broad outlines of his theory are still respected. R. H. Tawney is particularly acute in his recognition that Weber's emphasis on Calvinism is far too restrictive; he broadens the relevant influence to that of Puritanism. As Puritan thought developed, vigorous activity came to be regarded as a blessing in itself. This led in turn to the formation of a new species of capitalism, a system in which activity itself, not the wealth such activity produced, became the goal. Since Puritan sentiment was against indulgence in luxuries, this led to the reinvestment of earnings and to the further growth of the enterprises involved.

An entrepreneur thus motivated, who sought to appease his conscience by diligent and productive activity and yet who was prevented by that conscience from exulting in the fruits of his labor, was singularly vulnerable to the appeal of a theory such as mercantilism which exalted the busy traders as pillars of society. Tawney notes that "the main economic dogma of the mercantilist had an affinity with the main ethical dogma of the Puritan, which was the more striking because it was undesigned. To the former, production, not consumption, was the pivot of the economic system, and, by what seems to the modern reader a curious perversion, consumption is applauded only because it offers a new market for productive energies. To the latter, the cardinal virtues are precisely those which find in the strenuous toils of industry and commerce their most natural expression."[14]

Trevor-Roper undertakes a rigorous re-examination of Weber. In the first place, he points to the existence of capitalistic enterprises of the fifteenth century, mostly located in self-governing city-republics, which were as advanced in technique and scope of operations as those which were formed after the Reformation. Moreover, the practitioners of these enterprises tended to be "Erasmian," a type of pre-Protestant humanist who "extolls the real, inner piety of the active layman in his calling above the complacency of the indolent monks who assume a greater holiness because of the costume they wear or the 'mechanical devotions' which they practise." Then came the Counter-Reformation and persecution of Erasmians, many of whom fled to the Protestant countries and re-established their businesses there. "It was not that Calvinism created a new type of man who in turn created capitalism; it was rather that the old economic *elite* of Europe were driven into heresy because the attitude of mind which had been theirs for generations, was suddenly, in some places, declared heretical and intolerable."[15]

Trevor-Roper is undoubtedly correct in his assertion of the existence of large-scale capitalistic enterprises before the Reformation and of the existence of attitudes among the Erasmian Catholics which were similar to those of the sixteenth- and seventeenth-century Puritans. But while noting the qualitative similarity between the views of the two groups, we should not forget to emphasize the quantitative difference in the popular acceptance of the two generations of businessmen. The financiers and merchants of the fifteenth century were indeed tolerated by their sovereigns, but their activities were not expressly condoned by their Church. The practice of commerce, despite the wealth of many of the merchant-princes, often remained throughout the fifteenth century a *sub rosa* affair. By the seventeenth century, however, business had attained an unimpeachable moral character among Protestant peoples such as the English and the Dutch.

The principal elements in Puritan thought responsible for this shift in attitudes are: the increased emphasis upon internal discipline and individual responsibility for moral decision-making at the expense of the Catholic system of hierarchy and dogma; the Puritan stress upon the more restrictive virtues such as prudence, diligence, and thrift; and the development of the concept of the "calling" — a strenuous, life-long lay career to be undertaken with the same zeal and with the same hope of heaven as that followed by the cleric. Thus a merchant should approach his daily tasks with the same dedication as did his minister, and for the same reasons. When these elements were combined in an individual of some ability, he would obviously become a powerful force in the mercantile community. As is revealed in his *Meditations*, the youthful Defoe took his decision of whether to enter trade or the ministry quite seriously. His later difficulties in business were not the result of an insufficient belief in its importance but of a lack of prudence in his commercial dealings, and his career is a demonstration by negative example of the crucial importance of such "commercial" virtues as prudence and diligence.

The rise of Protestantism served ultimately to legitimize commerce and to strengthen businessmen for their demanding roles as agents of change in society. But without new attitudes toward the desirability of change, the process of legitimizing business might never have occurred. The modern notion of progress made its first appearance in the seventeenth century and dramatically changed the popular view of history.[16] Bacon may rightly be given responsibility for having the greatest single influence on this change of attitude. He insisted that the cyclical view of history propounded from ancient times to the Renaissance was not only wrong but damaging to humanity. Civilizations need not blindly rise and fall but could advance incrementally along a linear path. Progress, conceived as a steady advance toward a demonstrably improved state, was born.[17] Descartes' assertion of the superiority of reason over authority provided valuable assistance in this movement.

Bacon's goals for society were necessarily different from those of his predecessors, for the idea of progress is predicated upon the assumption that one can measure it. Art, virtue, self-knowledge, and most other ethical or aesthetic ideals do not lend themselves to measurement and therefore spawned vain and unresolvable disputes over whether the current age was superior or inferior to the previous one. For Bacon, the objectives worth discussing had to be scientific and technological, and the overriding test was their utility. If a particular development ameliorated the human state, if it produced better beer or better bread, it was an advancement.

By his formulation of the two books of God — the Bible and nature — Bacon was able to spare himself a good deal of controversy. The Bible, God's words, was a source of knowledge which deserved to be investigated, but in emphasizing God's words in the past, humankind had largely ignored nature, which is God's works. By studying nature one would come to know more of God. The emphasis, however, was not to be upon merely studying nature but in gaining control over it, with the aim of reducing nature to man's servant. The method to be employed was to be cooperative and cumulative; he felt that a number of experimenters working together and building upon each others' findings would give people control over their environment within a few generations.

The appeal of this system proved irresistible to a large number of Puritan as well as other thinkers, particularly in England. Its emphasis upon activity, public service, and educational reform found champions in such Puritans as Samuel Hartlib, John Durie, and J. A. Comenius, and there was a good deal of serious debate during the Commonwealth over the desirability of converting Oxford and Cambridge into trade schools. The feeling was abroad that the experimenter and the artisan, through their direct contact with the materials of nature, were more desirable species than was the speculative reasoner. One of the most striking, and certainly the most familiar, examples of the growing identification of the concerns of science and business is Sprat's *History of the Royal Society*, which continually stresses the practical and commercial results to be achieved by experimenters; Sprat even applauds Christ's choice of Apostles on the grounds that they were "men of *Honesty, Trades,* and *Business.*"[18] While Bacon's attitudes toward the new science may have stimulated a certain egalitarianism in some of his followers, Bacon himself did not view the merchant as the proper governor of a state, as he makes clear in his essay "Of Plantations."

Despite the heavy involvement of Puritans in science, it did not fall from favor at the Restoration, and many Puritan scientists were absorbed into the newly-formed Royal Society. Science and the belief in progress which it inspired were, like mercantilism, fast becoming the common property of all parties at the Restoration. The idea of progress is inherent in much mercantilist literature. The very aggressiveness which is central to most mercantilist thought is based upon a progressive habit of mind, as in this typical example: "these two [the fish and wool trades], are more than sufficient of themselves, if rightly managed, to employ all our poor, recruit our navy, bring us the wealth of the world, and make us the most potent and happy people under the sun."[19]

POLITICAL AND SOCIAL INCENTIVES

It may prove useful to inquire further into this spirit of aggressiveness which prevailed in the later seventeenth century. Puritanism, science, and mercantilism played a part, to be sure, but there were other more mundane forces which cooperated with these intellectual movements to produce progressive habits of mind. The Civil Wars, the plague, and the Great Fire of London had upset traditional social arrangements, leaving both London and the countryside severely disrupted. The Civil Wars seriously damaged the nobility and gentry as a group by diminishing their wealth, for on both sides great families freely melted down the plate they had accumulated over perhaps several generations in order to outfit military units of varying sizes. The decimation of the landed classes because of military casualties and the several confiscations of land during the wars put a large amount of real estate on the market and resulted in a great many new landed proprietors by the third quarter of the century.

The Great Plague had wreaked havoc particulary upon the artisans and laborers of London who were not equipped to flee the city, and the fire which may have put an end to the plague also destroyed much of Medieval London. During the later seventeenth century, London was rebuilt along modern lines. Wren's churches, the widened avenues, the Royal Exchange, and the Custom House provided a new and spacious setting for the indulgence of civic pride and the conduct of commercial affairs; the forces of scientific and commercial innovation had been strengthened by the social dislocations of mid-century.

There was a good deal of interplay between the owners of land and mercantile wealth. Landholders bought shares in commercial ventures, and merchants bought land. Some such merchants actually farmed the land, but many more bought country houses merely to escape occasionally from the City, while landlords might move into London townhouses to superintend their investments there. Marriages between City and county families would ultimately unite commercial and landed holdings, and the sons of the nobility and gentry were often apprenticed to merchants. The careers of two of the most prominent merchants of the seventeenth century, Sir Dudley North and Sir Josiah Child, will serve to illustrate similar processes of social interaction that were occurring in the seventeenth and eighteenth centuries.[20] Sir Dudley, the son of the fourth Lord North, was apprenticed to a merchant and made a fortune in the Turkey trade. Sir Josiah, the son of a wealthy merchant, prospered in the East India trade and bought Wanstead House, formerly the seat of the Earl of Leicester, whence he fled during the Great Plague of 1665; his son became the first Earl Tylney.

There were ample opportunities for intermarriage between landed and commercial interests. Gregory King estimates that in 1688 there were 3,000 Esquires with an average annual income of £450, 12,000 Gentlemen with £400, and 8,000 "Lesser merchants, traders by land" with £198. King also estimates that there were 50,000 shopkeepers and tradesmen in 1688 with an average income of £45.[21] There were undoubtedly numerous examples of businessmen with incomes between the averages he postulates, but he illustrates some important points about the mercantile community. First, there was a greater status attached to the overseas than to the internal trade and to the wholesale than to the retail trades, and secondly, there was a difference of an order of magnitude between the earnings of a prosperous merchant and those of a substantial shopkeeper. These facts help explain Defoe's chagrin at being termed a "hosier" or retailer by his political opponents when he was indeed a "hose factor," a wholesaler.

There was a great deal written during Defoe's lifetime about the usefulness and honor of business as an occupation, but the tone of such statements is generally defensive, illustrating that older aristocratic attitudes died hard. Steele insists in *Tatler* 207 that "The courtier, the trader, and the scholar should all have an equal pretension to the denomination of a gentleman," but it is clear that he feels that this was not the case in his day.[22] Despite the growing tendency toward the merging of landed and moneyed interests, most commercial writers, including Defoe, felt that the gentry both misunderstood and mistrusted the workings of trade. Lewes Roberts insisted in 1641 that trade "proveth beneficial to the nobility and gentry, by the improvement of their lands, by the sale and working of their coals, by the use of their timber, by the vent of their cattle, grain, and other provisions."[23] In 1718, William Wood was moved to express similar sentiments: "Can it possibly be believed hereafter, that so many of our nobility, clergy, gentry, and commonality, should not perceive the inseparable affinity between the *landed* and the *trading* interest, or give the preference of the *one* to the *other*, when it is demonstration [sic] that *it cannot go ill with TRADE but LAND will fall, nor ill with LAND but trade will feel it?*"[24] Wood felt he was baying in the wilderness, probably with some reason.

One of the more common defenses of the usefulness and propriety of trade as an occupation was in the obvious connection between the profits of the trader (particularly the overseas trader) and peace. Defoe himself was made sadly aware of this fact when he had a ship taken by the French privateers. John Evelyn makes this ironic point: "the most illustrious nations have esteemed the gain by traffic and commerce incompatible with *nobless*: not for being enemies to trade; but because they esteemed it an ignoble way of gain, *Quaestus Omnis indecorus Patribus*, says Livy, and were all for conquest and the sword."[25] Sir Dudley North insists more soberly that "it is peace, industry, and freedom that brings trade and wealth, and nothing else."[26] Not until the Walpole era could this pacific theory be tested, but according to Sir John Hawkins, speaking of the period 1710-1750, which takes him beyond Defoe's life span, peace produced striking results in England, which he described as a country where commerce and its concomitant luxury had been increasing, had given rise to new modes of living... the shopkeeper was transformed into a merchant, and the parsimonious stockbroker into a man of gallantry; the apron, the badge of mechanic operations, in all its varieties of stuff and colour, was laid aside; physicians and lawyers were no longer distinguishable by their garb; the former had laid aside the great wig, and the latter ceased to wear black, except in the actual exercise of their professions: in short, a few years of public tranquillity had transformed a whole nation into gentlemen.[27]

Hawkins at the end of the eighteenth century, like Steele at its beginning, states his case rather too ambitiously; yet it may be doubted that all the protestations of this sort, including those by Defoe, had as much effect in improving the status of businessmen as a few sketches of Sir Andrew Freeport in the *Spectator* or as a few marriages of City heiresses into county families.

This, in brief, was the economic and social milieu in which Defoe wrote. Mercantilism was the reigning economic philosophy, the middle classes were on the rise, there was a slight shift from agricultural to industrial production and a growth in output per unit of labor. More individuals were turning their creative energies to the problems of trade and manufacturing; the social stigma associated with participating in business affairs was waning, although some snobbish attitudes toward doing so remained. It was the most economically dynamic age so far in British history, but despite the incursions of civil war, plague, fire, and new fortunes made in trade, it did not represent a sharp break with the past. It was a time when risks and rewards were great; the merchant could enjoy his profits in a new country house while the bankrupt counted his losses in debtor's prison. Few men of his day would become more aware of the vagaries of commercial life than Defoe, and none would describe it so fully.

CHAPTER II

Defoe's Praise of Commerce

Perhaps the most striking aspect of Defoe's biography is his seeming lack of steadfastness. He ruined most of his business ventures through erratic political and literary zeal or through sheer imprudence. He proved willing to serve different political factions for a price and did not scruple to publish simultaneously conflicting opinions on various political issues of his day. Although he made great efforts to repay his creditors, he apparently, on occasion, defrauded his own family. As a secret government agent, a hired pen, and a fugitive from the law, intrigue and duplicity were his stock in trade. Seemingly unhampered by principle in so many of his concerns, he nevertheless chose to espouse the cause of trade steadfastly throughout his literary and journalistic career. True, there was no ready market for attacks on trade and thus no pecuniary temptation to attempt them, but it is remarkable that in reflecting upon his own chequered career as a merchant he chose to bless the opportunities which had increased his fortune rather than curse the fate which had repeatedly destroyed it.

His endorsement of the practice of business and his approval of those who participated in it are readily apparent in most of his literary work. In the novels this approval is occasionally explicit, as in Roxana's comment, "Sir Robert said, and I found it to be true, that a true-bred merchant is the best gentleman in the nation." In fact, as Samuel Macey points out, "Defoe is an evangelist in the special sense that relates to the accumulation of material wealth."[1] Often, however, such approval is merely implicit, as Maximillian Novak's observations on the structure of *Robinson Crusoe* demonstrate: Crusoe's misfortunes begin because he has disobeyed his father's wish that he go into trade, but he regains favor in the eyes of God as he develops the virtues of the merchant.[2] In Defoe's journalism and in his tracts on trade his approval of business is much less subtly expressed; statements such as the following soon cease to surprise the reader of Defoe's non-fiction:

> Not the variety of the climates, not the beauty of the heavenly bodies, not the influences of the elements in the productions of nature; not the harmony of the creation in general, or the wonderful operations of the parts in

particular, afford a more profitable, instructive, and diverting observation, than the pleasing diversity of nature, from whence is derived the foundations of commerce, and the chain of happy causes and consequences, which... embarked the whole world in a diligent application to TRADE.

(*Review*, IX. 110)

It would be impossible to maintain that Defoe does not occasionally attack various aspects and practices of business, but virtually all of these attacks are upon what he assumes to be dangerous or unproductive abuses of business, not upon business itself. Thus the "vices of our commerce grown upon us" which he enumerates are "stock-jobbing," "engrossings and monopolies," "the brewing and debauching of wines," and "high taxes or duties" (*Review*, VIII. 325-26). Rather than attacking business as a system which has produced these abuses, he attacks the abuses as threats to commercial prosperity. A description of Defoe's attitudes toward these real or imagined abuses provides an opportunity to discuss his abilities as an economic writer, a matter which should provide a useful prelude to an examination of his exalted attitude toward the rightful place which business should occupy in society.

DEFOE'S ECONOMIC THOUGHT

American history, unlike British experience which has tended to endorse state monopolies, has upheld Defoe's abhorrence of monopolistic practices through an extensive network of antitrust regulation. Defoe's vacillating attitudes toward trade in wine and other luxuries will be treated in some detail in our later discussion of his business ethics, but trade in luxuries is an issue which he certainly comprehended fully. His complaints about the relatively light taxes levied upon trade in his day, however, sound irretrievably quaint to twentieth-century observers accustomed not only to tariffs and excises but also to sizable taxes upon profits and to business's gradual provision of ever more substantial items of social overhead such as paid vacations, pensions, insurance, minority employment, and pollution abatement.

The worst that may be said of Defoe as an economic thinker is that he was at times reactionary, naive, and paternalistic. On each count, moreover, there are some slight extenuating circumstances. His dislike of the new-fangled methods of financing and his hatred of stock-jobbers, "those vermin of trade" (*Essay*, p. 28), is predicated upon his observation that tradesmen and merchants were likely to ruin their fortunes by investing in speculative stocks instead of gradually building up an estate through trade. *The Complete English Tradesman* abounds in warnings of the dangers of investing in securities. Defoe is hardly unique in his opinions of equities, however; eighteenth-century pamphlet literature abounds with anti-stock-jobbing tirades. The dangers he describes were indisputably real, but he is guilty of overlooking the significant advantages to commerce and manufacturing to be derived from well-regulated capital markets. Nor were stock-jobbers his only blind spot, for despite the many ingenious social proposals he advanced, such as "a tax upon Learning, to be paid by the authors of books" to support "idiots," he was unimaginative regarding the value of life insurance: "Insuring of life I cannot admire" (*Essay*, pp. 29, 21), although it must be pointed out that life insurance was in its infancy during his lifetime. Defoe was far from being a progressive in financial matters, even among seventeenth-century writers.[3]

Much of Defoe's naivete may be explained by the fact that modern economic thought had its beginnings during the Restoration; not only Defoe but most other contemporary writers were struggling to express concepts that have become second nature to later genertions. Thus we are surprised to come upon a lengthy passage in the *Plan* explaining that there are various qualities of goods and that they should fetch different prices, or to find a detailed summary in *The Complete English Tradesman* of the fact that the cost of goods varies from place to place because of the cost of transporting them. Doubtless an average newspaper reader of the twentieth century has a better grasp of the mathematical probabilities which form the basis of casualty insurance than does Defoe in his discussion "Of Friendly Societies" in the *Essay*. The lack of economic records, too, forced eighteenth-century writers to reason deductively on such matters as whether trade is increasing or decreasing. Therefore it will not do to be overly severe with Defoe as an economic commentator when he wrote under these difficulties.

Defoe at times revealed himself to be paternalistic, which puts him at odds with those who advocate free trade; nevertheless, mercantilism is itself inherently paternalistic. But this paternalism leads him to the justification of high prices and inefficiency. Defoe's oft-repeated conviction is "that the circulation of trade, like that of the blood, is the life of the commerce." To this end, he approves a large number of middlemen performing some slight operation on the goods they handle, thus raising the price to the final consumer by successive increments; the consumer of such goods then becomes a benefactor of full employment, and Defoe asserts on several occasions that the consumer should *enjoy* providing the nation with such a service.

This strange notion may have been unique with Defoe, but he was also one of the very few mercantilists who recognized the importance of the labor force as a market. He argued, contrary to ordinary mercantilist thought, that a well-paid labor force was an asset because it was able to consume more English manufactures than a poorly-paid force. His answer to the assertion that high labor costs would price English goods out of foreign markets was that well-paid labor produced better quality goods than did sweated labor and that the increase in quality more than offset the increase in price. His paternalism may have led him astray in his defense of inefficiency, but it also led him to a more just theory of human motivation than that held by many of his contemporaries. One of the best estimates of Defoe's technical ability remains that of his first major biographer:

> As a commercial writer, DeFoe is fairly entitled to stand in the foremost rank among his contemporaries, whatever may be their performances or their fame. Little would be his praise, to say of him, that he wrote on commercial legislation like Addison, who when he touches on trade, sinks into imbecility, without knowledge of fact, or power of argument. The distinguishing characteristics of DeFoe, as a commercial disquisitor, are originality and depth.... Were we to compare DeFoe with D'Avenant, it would be found, that D'Avenant has more detail from official documents; that DeFoe has more fact from wider inquiry.... But as a commercial prophet DeFoe must yield the palm to Child; who foreseeing from experience that men's conduct must finally be directed by their principles, foretold the colonial revolt... Were we however to form an opinion, not from special passages, but from whole performances, we must incline to DeFoe, when compared with the ablest contemporary.[4]

A more recent biographer maintains much the same view of Defoe's economic prowess: "There never was a more inquiring mind than his in all matters relating to trade and commerce, and he has hardly yet received the credit that is due to him as a distinguished amateur in the field of political economy." Or as Macey says, "He seems to take as his province virtually all mercantile experience in the known world."[5] Rarely indeed has a popular writer brought Defoe's blend of skill and enthusiasm to bear on economic matters. The economic historians, however, are somewhat less enthusiastic than Defoe's biographers on his merit as an economist and go only so far as to praise his accuracy of observation rather than his technical ability: "economic information is the one sort of information that Defoe seldom or never invents. He knew too much about it, and it interested him too much, to make it a suitable subject for promiscuous lying."[6]

Other than in his comments upon innovative practices or upon various abuses of commerce by unscrupulous traders, Defoe continually recommends business to his readers in terms of highest regard. Trade and manufacturing are decent, honorable, and important concerns because they are blessed by God and serve as defenders of the state; they are the nation's best stimulus to peace, best guarantee of victory in war, and best defense of liberty at home. Business also has the appeal of being a dynamic system, which though plied by businessmen yet improves the standard of living of all men and women, whether they are of the landed, laboring, professional, or trading classes; further, the businessman himself, if successful, not only increases his fortune and improves his status but also cultivates his mind through an association with trade. These are the fundamental claims that Defoe reiterates in favor of business; for the most part they represent a straightforward creed of decorous piety, mercantilistic ambition, and middle-class aspiration. The attributes of commerce which Defoe repeatedly emphasizes are its service to the state, by making the nation economically powerful; to civilization generally, by encouraging peace and fostering liberty; to all classes of society, by improving their standards of living; and to the businessman in particular, by improving his mind and increasing his social status: all with the approbation of God.

BUSINESS AS A SUPPORT OF GOD, STATE, AND CIVILIZATION

It is of some significance that Defoe did not feel compelled to undertake lengthy justifications of the righteousness of trade as a way of life. References to religious matters in his commercial tracts are generally so casual and underplayed as to indicate not only his complete lack of doubt of the virtuousness of trade as a calling but also the absence of any conception that the practices of trade might not be pleasing in God's sight. Chief among such references are his mention of Biblical figures as artisans or merchants, as in the comments that "honest Jubal and Tubal were the first *fiddle*-makers and *tinkers* in the world" or that "even *Solomon* had wanted gold to adorn the temple... if he had not turned Merchant-Adventurer, and sent his fleets to fetch it from the East Indies" (*Plan*, pp. 5, 10). In context, remarks such as these do not appear to be provoked by any allegations of the wickedness of trade. Defoe also has recourse to Scripture for the encouragement of Puritan virtues, as in: "*The diligent hand makes rich.* We know it is the hand of heaven that makes rich; but the text gives it to the hand of diligence, as if it were to encourage the man to application, and to bestir himself heartily; promising him both the advantage and credit of it, both the honour and the reward" (*CET*, II. 126). Or again: "Solomon was certainly a friend to men of business, as it appears by his frequent good advice to them. Prov. xviii. 9: he says, *he that is slothful in business is brother to him that is a great waster*: and in another place, *the sluggard shall be clothed in rags*, Prov. xxiii. 1" (*CET*, II. 31).

Occasionally the lesson is less formal, as in his recommendation of "forebearance to poor honest debtors": "even the best man, stands in need of the mercy of his Almighty creditor, and he should therefore show to his fellow-creature the mercy he every moment of his life has occasion to supplicate for himself" (*CET*, II. 115.) Defoe uses God's words both as a reminder that Biblical figures were not above involvement in trade and as an exhortation to diligent application; he also makes reference to God's works, the world, and expounds his belief that God has separated nations by water and has distributed different native commodities to each in order to unite them by the workings of commerce: as sin has separated nations, so commerce shall reunite them. It is this belief which is behind his contention that "Providence concurs in, and seems to have prepared the world for commerce" (*Review*, IX. 108). Because "it is the hand of heaven that makes rich," success in mercantile endeavor signifies divine grace, and because "Providence concurs in" commerce, the merchant may well be a kind of favored agent of God's will.

Just as there is nothing in trade inimical to religion, so much so indeed that God may have taken steps to foster commerce, there is nothing harmful to the nation in the workings of trade:

> I divide the care and concern of the nation among these generals, religion, constitution, and commerce; trade, as it is the last of these three, is the first of all the subsequent concerns of the kingdom, and I rank it hand in hand with religion and constitution, not by way of equality, but as it is the great auxiliary, which enables us to protect, defend and preserve the other from all its opposers. (*Review*, IV. 588)

If God has been so farsighted as to prepare the world for trade, Defoe seems to intimate, should not man be prudent enough to follow His example, by disposing the state for the practice of commerce? Besides, descending to a more mundane level, "Trade pays two thirds of our taxes" (*Review*, VIII. 25),[7] and "'tis the longest purse that conquers now, not the longest sword" (*Plan*, p. 39); it would seem that God helps those who help themselves. Trade is at the very heart of England's affairs; Defoe insists that

> England is a trading nation, that the wealth and opulence of the nation, is owing to trade, that the influence of trade is felt in every branch of its government, in the value of its land, and the blood of gallantry, so that trade is the life of the nation, the soul of its felicity, the spring of its wealth, the support of its greatness, and the staff on which both kings and people lean, and which (if it should sink) the whole fabric must fall, the body politick would sicken and languish, its power decline, and the figure it makes in the world, grow by degrees, most contemptibly mean. (*Review*, II. 9)

This contention that trade is the chief support of civilization could be applied not only to the national affairs of England but to the condition of the whole world as well; trade has the potential to transform not only England but all nations on earth:

> Trade is the wealth of the world; trade makes the difference as to rich or poor, between one nation and another; trade nourishes industry, and industry begets trade; trade disperses the natural wealth of the world, and trade raises new species of wealth, which nature knew nothing of: trade has two daughters, whose fruitful progeny in arts may be said to employ mankind; namely,
>
> MANUFACTURE
AND
NAVIGATION.
>
> ... To conclude, manufacture for employment at home, and navigation for employment abroad, both together, seem to set the busy world at work; they seem to join hands to encourage the industrious nations, and if well managed, infallibly make the world rich. (*Plan*, pp. 51-52)

Two of the great claims for trade are that it can make both England and the rest of the world rich. Defoe makes both of these claims and struggles to reconcile their implications. Further complicating his task are two other potentially conflicting assertions — that trade both makes nations powerful and encourages them to live peacefully with one another. These various claims may be just, of course, but Defoe's difficulty was in combining them in a theoretical system intellectully acceptable to seventeenth- and eighteenth-century England. Industry and commerce had increased England's wealth and power; that was an observable fact. They had had the same effect upon other nations, noticeably France and Holland. And while commercial disputes might become national causes which contributed to declarations of war, clearly the merchant had much to lose during the unsettled conditions of wartime, as Defoe himself discovered upon losing a ship to French privateers. The implicit system which seems to emerge from Defoe's commercial writings is that the conflicts between England's growing power and that of the rest of the world and between the ability of trade to increase power and to stimulate peace might be successfully resolved if *England* managed to stay richer and more powerful than its neighbors.

This whole peace-power line of reasoning is a tortured and discontinuous one in Defoe. He insists that England, as a rich nation, has no incentive to provoke wars, for "poverty and want raise soldiers. Trade is a friend to peace, and provides for the people a far better way: trade sets them to work for their bread, not to fight for it; and if we want men in England, 'tis not that the number is deficient, but because they live too well to go for soldiers" (*Plan*, p. 74). Furthermore, England is rich not because of war but because of trade: "the greatness of the British nation is not owing to war and conquests, to enlarging dominions by the sword, or subjecting the people of other countries to our power; but it is all owing to trade, to the increase of our commerce at home, and extending it abroad" (*CET*, I. 249). Thus trade makes a people rich, and riches dispose a people to peaceful behavior.

But there is another side as well: "The advantages gained by the war with Spain, gave England such a start of her neighbors in this single reign, in matters of commerce, as the whole world could never overtake her in to this day" (*Plan*, p. 105). Defoe also maintains that "money raises armies, and trade raises money; and so it may be truly said of trade, that it makes princes powerful, nations valiant, and the most effeminate people that can't fight for themselves, if they have but money, and can hire other people to fight for them, they become as formidable as any of their neighbors" (*Plan*, p. 40). There is money to be made during wartime, of course:

> though there are a great many families raised within a few years, in the late war, by great employments and by great actions abroad, to the honour of the English gentry, yet how many more families among the tradesmen have been raised to immense estates, even during the same time, by the attending circumstances of the war; such as the clothing, the paying, the victualling and furnishing, &c. (*CET*, I. 243)

Defoe admits that war provides commercial advantages which finance armies to fight more wars which are on occasion profitable.

These contradictory notions crop up continually in Defoe's works.

For the most part he appears content merely to praise both the martial and the pacific attributes of trade without attempting to reconcile them. Notice, however, that in either case it is trade which supplies the capability and which receives the blessing as a force for either war or peace. Defoe does hint at a resolution of these seemingly contradictory attributes of trade in the fact that England is herself basically benign: "*England*, happy in herself, seeks no living abroad, nor dominion abroad; give her peace and trade, she is the happiest, and will be the richest, and in time the most populous nation in the world" (*Review*, IV. 403). Thus while both war and peace can in various ways promote trade and increase wealth, once a preponderance of wealth and power is vested in Britain, she, with her fundamentally peace-loving impulses, would have every incentive to force peace upon the rest of the world:

> England is possessed of such a vast wealth, both in trade, people, and dominion, that she wants nothing to secure her being the greatest nation in the world; but peace — Union at home, and *peace abroad*, is all she wants; other nations may thrive by rapine, and devastation, invading others and tyrannizing at home; but *England* thrives best by *peace*. (*Review*, III. 278)

This line of reasoning is based upon two assumptions: one which Defoe's English audience might readily grant, the basic benignity of the English people; and one which they might earnestly hope to be true, the superior wealth of England.

However England might have originally achieved a position of commercial dominance, whether through war or peace or merely through fortuitous circumstances, if the nation had indeed become the most commercially-advanced nation of the world, it alone of the nations of the world would have the most to lose by war. Further, as most mercantilists taught, recourse to arms was not necessary even to build an empire; a commercial nation could gain more through colonization and trade than through costly campaigns. A highly-developed commercial nation also had more to lose in war than did more primitive states. Simply stated, the financial return to the premier commercial power was greater from peace than from war.

For a writer such as Defoe who believed ardently that England's future greatness was dependent upon commercial prosperity, it became important to stress the extent of the nation's present mercantile achievement. He wrote a vast amount on this subject, and as James Sutherland has said of him, "He comes nearest to being a poet when he writes in impassioned prose about the expansion of English commerce." John

McVeagh goes further, maintaining that "Defoe's commercial writings ... hard-headed as they are, are nevertheless shot through by a vision — one can call it no less—of the beauty and excellence of creation; and this strong idealising apprehension lies behind his particular schemes of gain, fortifying and sustaining their otherwise crudely materialistic arguments."[8] Defoe argues that "It is no vain boast, nor any unjust partiality to ourselves to say, that England is at this time not only a nation of the greatest trade in the world, but that it is the center of the whole commerce of Europe, if not of the whole trading world" (*CET*, II. 158). Furthermore, "no nation can undersell the English in their manufactures" (*Review*, II. 61); "the English man's work, according to his wages, out-weigh [that of other nationalities]; as his beer is strong, so is his work" (*Plan*, p. 30); and "the working manufacturing people of England, eat the fat, drink the sweet, live better, and fare better than the working poor of any other nation in Europe" (*CET*, I. 252). So far as Defoe could have proved, these probably were indeed "vain boasts"; England was easily among the leaders as a commercial nation, but contemporary economic data were too scarce for Defoe to have made rigorous comparisons between shipping volumes and national standards of living.[9]

Defoe at times frankly revealed this lack of hard data in statements such as "The commerce of England, is an immense and almost incredible thing, and ... we must content ourselves with being in some cases in a difficulty as to numbers and figures" (*Plan*, p. 81), or "We may venture to say in public, that we are a most powerful nation in shipping, having the greatest number of ships and seamen, of any nation in the world, without being able to give a particular account how many ships we have, or how many seamen we employ" (*Plan*, p. 80). By usually writing more authoritatively ("we are the greatest trading country in the world" [*CET*, I. 243]) Defoe is able to establish his position that the volume of England's traffic is a matter of international prestige (and should therefore be nurtured) and that England's merchants and tradesmen are engaged in a highly patriotic undertaking (and should therefore be respected). The businessman in Defoe's eyes has become a benefactor of society.

COMMERCE AND INDUSTRY: BENEFACTORS OF ALL CLASSES

Occasionally Defoe presents the merchant's service to society as being intensely dramatic: "There was, one year of the late war with France, a very terrible scarcity of corn throughout the whole kingdom of France, such a scarcity, that, had it not been for the merchants, who, as we might say, rummaged the world for corn, many thousands of people must have perished more than did" (*Plan*, p. 71). Even more important is the role he ascribes to trade and to the tradesman in securing liberty for Englishmen. Defoe expresses this view of history: in the Medieval period, "People were divided into master and servant; not landlord and tenant, but the lord and the vassal" (*Plan*, p. 34). Because of the introduction of trade ("I insist upon it, that trade alone made the difference" [*Plan*, p. 35]), people were able to barter their labor in a relatively free market and gain some measure of self-sufficiency: "Trade, brought a revolution in the very nature of things; the poor began to work, not for cottages and liveries, but for money, and to live, as we say, at their own hands" (*Plan*, p. 36). Thus trade begets liberty. Liberty, for its part, in turn begets more trade, for "Liberty makes nations thrive, people great, a country pleasant, ay, and nature fruitful; for liberty encourages industry, sloth and slavery go hand in hand, and encourage one another" (*Review*, III. 671).

Besides being instrumental in providing liberty, trade had produced significant economic benefits for all classes in England, and Defoe seemingly never tires of announcing that "Trade is the life of the world's prosperity, and all the wealth that has been extraordinary, whether of nations or of cities, has been raised by it" (*Plan*, p. 24). Because of this service which trade supplies, we should be grateful to businessmen: "trade is a public benefit; and, in a word, the wealth of families, the rates of lands, and the strength of the nation, depend all upon trade. As trade then is a public benefit, the tradesmen are a public blessing..." (*CET*, II. 99). Commerce deserves England's protection because it has done much for its people and has the power to do yet more:

> the wealth, the glory, the great families, and the essence of this nation *as a people*, had their original in trade; I think, I need not tell you now that to preserve all these, there is no human concern can rationally equal that of our care, to preserve, increase, and support our commerce.
>
> (*Review*, IV. 587-88).

The nobility and gentry have particularly benefited from the good offices of trade, and "England may, without any reproach to her, be said to be *a trading nation*... her numerous gentry, her illustrious nobility, and most, if not all her best families, owe their wealth and rise, first or last, to the opulence and profits of trade" (*Review*, II. 9). The economic benefit from trade which accrues to the landed interests is in the form of increased rents: "As the numbers of people increase, the consumption of provision increases; as the consumption increases, the rate or value will rise at market; and as the rate of provisions rises, the rents of land rise: so the gentlemen are with the first to feel the benefit of trade, by the addition to their estates" (*Plan*, p. 13). This is very calmly and very well said, but Defoe often undercuts his own arguments by the shrill note of hysteria which he allows to creep into his discourse. The appeal to fear is one of his most frequent devices, particularly in the *Review*, and he uses it repeatedly when addressing the landed classes and detailing their benefits from trade: this is unfortunate for his purpose because in doing so he reveals his lack of a power position. By departing from sober argument he shows himself to be unsure of his own ground and in awe of the upper class, even when he is attempting to prove that trade is, in fact, no adversary to it but the source and the preserver of its prosperity:

> The foundation of our prosperity I take to lie in our trade, we were raised from nothing by it, and we shall be reduced to nothing when we lose it; we have few families so great or so ancient, but they have either begun in trade; or increased and received additions from trade; and if any are so vain as to condemn that original, *let them tell us*, what their estates would be worth, if the increase of trade, which always adds to the value of land, had not raised their rents and what they would come to, should a decay of trade reduce them to their very poor original. (*Review*, IV. 584)

While the landed classes benefit from improved trade indirectly through increased rents, labor benefits more directly from it, as we have seen. Defoe points out, however, that the poor have a Job's choice in the matter, mentioning by way of example that "the Mahometans, have little or no hand in it [trade]; they abhor business and labour, and despise industry, and they starve accordingly" (*Plan*, p. 11). Just as Defoe is often shrill in his proclamations of the benefits the landed classes reap from trade, he is frequently harsh in his predictions of the dire consequences of sloth among the laboring poor. His comments on labor nevertheless seem somewhat calmer than his assaults upon landed gentlemen partly because he is not violating the hierarchical pecking order in lecturing the poor but also because he fortifies his discourse with a heavy dose of conventional Puritan ethic:

> Poverty is the fountain of all manner of idleness; thay have in short nothing to do, no employment in which they can get their bread by their labour; their work gets no wages for want of labour; diligence promotes trade, and trade encourages diligence; labour feeds trade, and trade feeds the labourer.
>
> (*Plan*, pp. 24-25)

Again:

> The diligent trading manufacturing world work cheerfully, live comfortably; they sing at their labour, work by their choice, eat and drink well, and their work goes on pleasantly, and with success: whereas the unemployed world groan out their souls in anguish and sorrow, not by their work, but for want of it; and sink, as I may justly say, under the weight of their idleness and sloth. (*Plan*, p. 29)

Here is ritual praise of one of the "commercial virtues" enumerated by Tawney and Weber, and here too, in the contrast between the comfortable worker and the unhappy idler, is the text which Hogarth was later to illustrate in his "Industry and Idleness."

At times Defoe could emphasize the rewards of trade to workers without recourse to the complementary problem of the punishment of sloth: "Trade invigorates the world, gives employment to the people, raises pay for their labour, and increases that pay as their labour increases, and as their performance excels." Indeed, "the great end of trade" is "the supporting our manufactures, and the employing our poor" (*Plan*, p. 33). Thus, at least in one sense, the entire economic system seems designed for the support of the poor. That trade did not always receive *their* support is seen by Defoe's occasionally-expressed desire "to make laws to oblige them to work" (*Review*, IV. 595). This latter sentiment hardly squares with Defoe's earlier-mentioned insistence on the role of trade in promoting liberty for all classes; he can hardly be classed as a thorough-paced libertarian. Such conflicts as these are typical of Defoe's general attitude toward commerce; he may contradict himself on various matters relating to trade, but he does not denigrate trade itself. In this case, he both defends trade as a preserver of liberty and recommends a curtailment of liberty to promote trade. Despite Defoe's frequent recitations of the dangers of sloth and his occasional suggestions that work be made compulsory, he repeatedly insists that English labor works harder and earns more than its counterparts abroad: "It would appear, that the English poor earn more money than the same class of men or women can do at the same kind of work, in any other nation. Nor will it be denied but that they do more work also..." (*Review*, IV. 39).

While the rewards of commerce to the laboring and landed classes are primarily the economic ones of wages and rents, the trading classes receive not only economic profits but educational and social benefits as well. Defoe presents the educational benefits as matters of practical training in academic disciplines and in virtue. Occasionally he states his position modestly: "Though it is not absolutely necessary that every tradesman should be a philosopher, yet every tradesman, in his way, knows something that even a philosopher may learn from" (*CET*, I. 28). Often he expounds more freely on this theme: "A merchant sitting at home in his counting-house, at once converses with all parts of the known world. This, and travel, makes a true-bred merchant the most intelligent man in the world, and consequently the most capable..." (*Essay*, p. 7). Defoe repeatedly emphasizes the practical and cosmopolitan knowledge acquired by the man of affairs in preference to the learning acquired in schools:

> His [the merchant's] learning excels the mere scholar in Greek and Latin, as much as that does the illiterate person that cannot write or read. He understands languages without books, geography without maps; his journals and trading voyages delineate the world; his foreign exchanges, protests, and procurations speak all tongues; he sits in his counting-house and converses with all nations, and keeps up the most exquisite and extensive part of human society in a universal correspondence. (*Review*, III. 7)

Defoe, typically, is on solid Baconian ground here but, alas for his argument, he is also typically himself in undermining his position by suggesting that trade may be indeed *antithetical* to formal learning: "I easily acknowledge myself blockhead enough to have lost the fluency of expression in the Latin, and so far trade has been prejudice to me" (*Review*, II. 149). Yet he occasionally embellishes his writing with Latin tags as if to prove the contrary position.

The chief virtues which Defoe finds to be taught by trade are two pillars of the Puritan ethic, thrift and diligence. Trade positively conditions one to live within one's means: "There is something so absurd in a life of imprudent expense, that a man bred in business can never fall into it, unless he has first forfeited all his former capacities, and is no more able to make any judgment of things" (*CET*, II. 134). Too, "the diligent tradesman never tires" (*Plan*, p. 88), even when faced with adversity, for "as long as he can struggle he may hope. A tradesman is the best fitted to struggle with disasters of any part of mankind; give him but liberty and something to begin with, he will not fail to engage in something or other that will turn to account" (*CET*, II. 125). All this diligence, furthermore, is constructive and wholesome, as Defoe attempts to illustrate in the *Plan* (pp. 227-33) by his contrast of the Spanish and English methods of colonization. The Spaniards, he points out, got to America first, seized the most fruitful lands, massacred the inhabitants, and began shipping home gold and silver. The English came later and found no silver and gold but a rather more barren and inhospitable clime which through peaceful and diligent application to commerce they managed to make more valuable than the mines of Mexico and Peru. Trade, Defoe seems to say, is a hard and virtuous master which through a series of wholesome incentives tends to improve the moral tone not only of its followers, but of the society in which they ply their trade.

But for Defoe, of course, virtue is far from being its sole reward; the wealth and social position which flow to the successful merchant are vastly more enthralling. As Michael Shinagel has said of a different set of Defoe's works, "The flat quality of Defoe's religious writings contrasts sharply with the enthusiasm of his writings on business. He simply could not project himself into the role of preacher and religious instructor with quite the same 'gust' as he could act the role of apostle of trade and apologist of the middle class."[10] Shinagel's important exposition of Defoe's thoughts on social aspirations and rewards makes him the undisputed expert on the subject, and little remains to be said here except to refer the reader to him and to supplement his rather sparse treatment of Defoe's occasionally contradictory statements on the social position of the tradesman or merchant.

It would be misleading to say that Defoe's writings on these matters are ambiguous. In his expository works he is one of the most unambiguous and straightforward writers in English literary history. On the other hand, he is often contradictory, so that his *position* may be said to be ambiguous. Consider these comments on Charles II, both from *The Complete English Tradesman*:

> King Charles II, who was perhaps the prince of all the kings that ever reigned in England, who best understood the country and the people he governed, used to say, that the tradesmen were the only gentry in England. (I. 242)

> Who would have lent King Charles II, 50 £ on the credit of his own word or bond, after the shutting up the Exchequer? The royal word was made a jest of, and the character of the king was esteemed a fluttering trifle, which no man would venture his money upon. (I. 276)

This is an inconsistency utterly in character for Defoe. He reveres Charles for praising tradesmen and reviles him for interrupting trade; Defoe is here inconsistent in his attitude toward Charles, but consistent in his attitude toward trade. As with so many of Defoe's inconsistencies, he may contradict his own statement about trade, but he virtually never denigrates trade itself.

THE BUSINESSMAN'S SOCIAL STANDING

But while Defoe seems to be supremely confident of the importance of commerce to society, he apparently does have some doubts about the proper social standing of the merchant. His two chief methods of describing the social position of businessmen (and the vast majority during this period were indeed men) are to declare with great certainty that the merchant is of the highest station, and to hedge by maintaining that this station pertains only to *English* rather than foreign tradesmen or to merchants rather than "mere mechanics" or, finally, to the *sons* of merchants rather than to the merchants themselves. After encountering Defoe's ebullient certainty on the value of commerce to the nation and to all its people, it is perhaps surprising to find him faltering on the crucial point of the merchant's acceptance by that society. His hesitation may be explained in part by the fact that much of his praise for trade itself is couched in terms of what it will do for England in the future, while the problem of social standing is one which takes place in the immediate present. Defoe's devotion to commerce, furthermore, is a matter of belief; the acceptance or rejection of merchants into high levels of contemporary society was a matter of observable fact.

An interesting feature of Defoe's discussions of the social station of businessmen is that he rarely makes a hierarchical distinction between the status of merchants and tradesmen: both may aspire to be gentlemen, and both seem to have the same difficulties in achieving their aspirations. Defoe can be very emphatic about the high station of the merchant, as for instance in the *Review*: "How many now illustrious families, have their modern original from the oppulency of trade; and the merchant we find, stands as fair for a peer as another man, and if wealthy enough, appears every jot as well qualified for that dignity" (*Review*, III. 38). To be sure, Defoe makes quite clear that it is only the tradesman or merchant of substance who deserves this elevation: trade

> is certainly the most noble, most instructive, and improving of any way of life. The artificers or handicraftsmen, are indeed slaves; the gentlemen are

the plowmen of the nation, but the merchant is the support, and improver of power, learning, and fortunes. (*Review*, III. 6)

Defoe's most frequent modification of the ideal of the merchant-gentleman is in reserving the social prestige of a gentleman for *English* businessmen. This is utterly in keeping with the tenor of his writings on trade itself, and he devotes portions of *The Complete English Tradesman* to that purpose.

Just as the trade of England is greater than that of other states, so are her tradesmen: "the English tradesman may be allowed to rank with the best gentlemen in Europe; and, as the prophet Isaiah said of the merchants of Tyre, that *her traffickers were the honorable of the earth,* Isa. xxiii.8" (*CET*, I. 248). While the quotation from Scripture hardly seems to exclude Continental tradesmen from social favor, Defoe makes clear his own intention to do so: "The word 'tradesman,' in England, does not sound so harsh as it does in other countries; and to say a gentleman-tradesman, is not so much nonsense as some people would persuade us to reckon it" (*CET*, I. 248). In short, "trade in England neither is or ought to be leveled with what it is in other countries" (*CET*, I. 247).

Despite the fact that, as Samuel Macey observes, "the endeavour to upgrade the status of the bourgeoisie permeates Defoe's works,"[11] and despite the fact that wealth is the crucial characteristic of gentility in Defoe's social vision, even in *The Complete English Tradesman*, devoted in large part to inflating the self-esteem of tradesmen as a class, Defoe makes two important reservations about the entrance of English tradesmen into the fraternity of gentlemen. In the first place, there are other requisite qualities beside sheer wealth; certain manners must be adopted, and the former tradesman must never appear "purse-proud" or niggardly (*CET*, II. 148-52). Furthermore, the merchant or tradesman may have to be content with merely establishing his progeny as gentlemen:

> Trade is so far here from being inconsistent with a gentleman, that, in short, trade in England makes gentlemen, and has peopled this nation with gentlemen; for, after a generation or two, the tradesman's children, or at least their grandchildren, come to be as good gentlemen, statesmen, parliamentmen, privy-counselors, judges, bishops, and noblemen, as those of the highest birth and the most ancient families. (*CET*, I. 246)

Defoe puts this distinction, that it is the progeny of the businessman, not necessarily the businessman himself, who rise in society, at the heart of *The Complete English Gentleman,* which Shinagel rightly terms "the capstone to his treatment of gentility."[12] Here the tradesman is no longer described in the glowing terms of *The Complete English Tradesman,* but his sons may still aspire to gentility:

> the successors to, and sons of, the overrich scoundrel, call him as you will, become gentlemen and are without hesitation received for such among the best families in Britain; nor do any of the most ancient families scruple to form alliances with them by intermarriages, or esteem their blood at all dishonored by the conjection. (*CEG*, pp. 258-59)

This "scoundrel" who has founded the house is inappropriate for consideration as a gentleman because he probably "can no more leave off the ravening after money, *Fas aut nefas,* than an old thief can leave off pilfering, or an old whore leave off procuring" (*CEG*, p. 258). Having gone this far in caricaturing the retired merchant, however, Defoe will not go further to allow that there is anything inherently debasing in the pursuit of trade:

> We see abundance of tradesmen who derived from families of the best gentry in the nation: whether our nicer observers of the untainted blood of families, as they call it, will pretend that such men lose the claim which they had before to the name of gentleman and are, being once leveled with the meaner people always of the rank with them ... still their having been merchants or factors or tradesmen, wholesale or retail, did not cut off the entail of blood any more than it cut off the surnames. (*CEG*, pp. 264-65)

When praising commerce, Defoe could write as if successful merchants were automatically absorbed into the gentry; when analyzing society, however, he was forced to admit that the process was difficult and might take a couple of generations to complete. Commerce, as an abstract cause or as a beneficial force in the culture, might seize his imagination and generate limitless visions of future prosperity and endless justifications of its present performance, but when he turned to the contemporary situation of the businessman he was forced by his observation of social realities to recognize that economic aspirations were more easily assuaged than social ones.

A final appeal of commerce for Defoe is its dynamic nature: "An estate's a pond, but trade's a spring" (*CET*, I. 245). Not only the end products of commercial activity—wealth, power, national prestige, support of the poor—but the *process* of accumulation fascinated him:

"The merchant makes a wet bog become a populous state; enriches beggars, ennobles mechanics, raises not families only, but towns, cities, provinces and kingdoms" (*Review*, III. 7).[13] For Defoe, the very activity of the busy merchant held a temperamental appeal which was sanctioned by his Puritan background: "Employment is life, sloth and indolence is death; to be busy, is to be cheerful, to be pleasant; to have nothing to do, is all dejection, dispiriting, and in a word to be fit for nothing but mischief and the devil" (*Plan*, p. 52). The career of a tradesman was apt to be a struggle, and Defoe views this struggle as a heroic one; nor can we fail to see a reference to his own mercantile career in this description of the tradesman's rise from bankruptcy:

> To fall, is common to all mankind; to fall and rise is a particular few men arrive to; but to fall into the very dirt of scandal and reproach, and rise with reputation; to fall with infamy and rise with applause; to fall detested, and rise caressed and embraced by all mankind; this, I think, is a kind of 'peculiar' to the tradesman, nay, to the unhappy, unfortunate tradesman, who, by this one turn of affairs, is lifted out of the mire into a station of life infinitely superior to the best condition he was ever in before.
> (*CET*, II. 130-31)

Perhaps it was this attraction to the dynamic nature of commerce which made Defoe its champion and which led him to be loyal to it as a cause, even after he had suffered a great deal from its swings of fortune. True, if it were not for trade in the first place, he never would have had his prosperous days at all, but how very rational and unlike Defoe to think so calmly about trade, particularly when his commercial downfalls seem to have been caused by nothing more than his own rashness. Whatever the reason, he hardly ever ventured to castigate trade itself, even while he routinely contradicted himself in defending it. He had difficulties reconciling his claims that trade promoted peace with his claims that trade bolstered defense, but these were standard mercantilistic tenets which do have a certain logical appeal: one may altruistically desire a system which removes the incentives for warfare, but it is hardly responsible, in the light of history, to expect such a system to work.

He had further problems working out his thoughts on the merchant's place in society, and here he ran himself into more glaring contradictions. He viewed the merchant as a benefactor of society, and his frustration upon recognizing that the culture undervalued the businessman's services drove Defoe to address the nobility and gentry shrilly on this point. Despite his contradictions and frustrations, however, he developed a vision of commerce as an undertaking of the greatest consequence. Through the course of his voluminous writings on trade he consistently described it as a system pleasing to God's sight whereby men might actively engage with fortune for their own self-improvement, for the benefit of all classes of people, and for the ultimate good of the state. Much of what Defoe wrote is not original with him; the extent of his achievement as a defender of commerce is to be measured by the volume of material he produced and by the fact that this notoriously changeable man chose to remain steadfast to this particular cause throughout his lengthy and turbulent literary career.

CHAPTER III

Defoe's *Tour* as a Paean of Business

Of his many economic works, Defoe's *Tour* is his most comprehensive and successful apologia for business. Narrated at a seemingly leisurely pace, it lacks the strident tone of much of the *Review*. Written ostensibly on Britain rather than on business, it avoids as well the appearance of special pleading so evident in *A Plan of the English Commerce* and contains less pedantic detail (such as bookkeeping lessons) than *The Complete English Tradesman*. It also is less ambiguous on the worth of commerce than is his fiction; although Defoe's praise of trade echoes through his novels, *Robinson Crusoe* has, after all, been cited in support of Karl Marx perhaps as often as of Max Weber or Adam Smith.

Any analysis of Defoe's praise of commerce might well treat his *Tour* as merely another of his major works dealing with business, for in it he repeats most of the claims for the importance and dignity of commerce that he insists upon elsewhere. Yet two considerations compel giving it special treatment: its comparative neglect by scholars and its singularly successful defense of business. Godfrey Davies wrote in 1950 that "None of the longer works of Defoe has received so little actual attention as the *Tour*,"[1] and except for an illuminating but all too brief treatment of the *Tour* by Michael Shinagel in 1968, and the extensive and admirable work of Pat Rogers, this largely remains the case today. Rogers himself notes that some of Defoe's biographers "ignore [the *Tour*] altogether."[2] Such neglect is easily understood; a guide book is inevitably one of the most topical and practical of literary genres, and as its age increases its utility must necessarily diminish. While it remained current, however, Defoe's *Tour* evidently enjoyed a wide audience, for it went through nine heavily-edited editions between its initial publication in 1724-27 and 1778, after which time it was not again reprinted until the twentieth century.

By the late eighteenth century, the *Tour* evidently was considered to be out of date. In the half-century since the first appearance of his volumes, the face of Great Britain had changed significantly enough to limit their usefulness as a travel guide. Their eclipse might be due in part to another cause, however: the *attitudes* Defoe expressed might well have begun to seem outmoded. At the time of the *Tour*'s original publication, Pope's *Windsor Forest*, Thomson's *Seasons*, and the works of the georgic poets had begun to celebrate the potential beneficence of business; fifty years later, with the Industrial Revolution more obviously under way, literary opinion had begun its shift toward Blake's characterization of industry as "dark satanic mills." (George Barringer ventures the opinion that "as English economics became concerned with production rather than trade, interest in [the *Tour*] declined."[3]) The *Tour* would have been particularly vulnerable to a shift in popular values, for it is as much a catalogue of Defoe's attitudes toward business as it is a collection of geographical facts about Britain. The facts of terrain and climate and custom are mere starting points in Defoe's description; he is not so much interested in describing the anatomy of England as in detailing its physiology and in making pronouncements upon the health of the various parts. For Defoe, of course, the processes most worth detailing are economic ones, and the objective geographical facts are but the skeleton which lend structure to his succession of comments upon commercial matters.

Macey describes the *Tour* as "essentially a guide to social and economic conditions," and Shinagel notes that "Defoe saw in miniature the mighty industrial empire of Macaulay's age. Despite the difference in their eras, they both had the same vision of England."[4] It is this vision which transforms Defoe's travel book into a powerful piece of pro-business propaganda. Shinagel is perhaps not so conscious of the pervasive influence of Defoe's outlook in the *Tour* as he might be, however, for he also states that "In the *Tour* Defoe dealt with this favorite theme [middle-class gentility] factually, not imaginatively."[5] Here Shinagel makes a distinction between Defoe's treatment of this theme in his fiction and in the *Tour*. Certainly there are differences between Defoe's handling of the theme of middle-class gentility (and of the other themes which constitute his defense of commerce as well) in the novels and the *Tour*. Most importantly, in the *Tour* he is free to devote more space to economic matters without the necessity of developing plot, character, and the other requisites of the novelist's art. Nevertheless, it is misleading to suggest that in writing the *Tour*, Defoe was sacrificing imagination to facts. The mere presence of a vast amount of factual detail need not be accepted as prima-facie evidence in this case, for it has long been noted that one of the greatest beauties of his fiction is his masterful and copious use of circumstantial detail. If his use of such detail in his novels did not preclude his treating their subjects imaginatively, it need not have hampered his imaginative vision in his travel journal. The least that may be maintained is that the format of the *Tour* gives a rather freer rein to his imagination than is allowed by the argumentative tenor of such baldly economic works as the *Plan* and the *Review* or the instructional nature of *The Complete English Tradesman*.

In most of his other works on business, Defoe was constrained by his need to write to the moment and to search out examples which would prove his particular points. In the *Tour*, ostensibly with no point to prove and no ax to grind, he could merely record whatever data appealed to him and go on to describe the particular refraction of Britain which corresponded to his own world view. In his other commercial works he might choose to argue that trade should be considered the most crucial of worldly undertakings or that the world should grant greater respect to the merchant. In the *Tour*, however, he need only describe communities dependent upon trade and rewards showered upon tradesmen to give the impression that life actually proceeded along these lines. In a work such as the *Plan*, Defoe was limited to asserting that

> the manufacturing counties are calculated for business, the unemployed counties for pleasure; the first are thronged with villages and great towns, the last with parks and great forests; the first are stored with people, the last with game; the first are rich and fertile, the last waste and barren; the diligent part of the people are fled to the first, the idler part are left at the last; in a word, the rich and thriving tradesmen live in the first, the decaying wasting gentry in the last. (*Plan*, pp. 67-68)

In the *Tour*, however, he could demonstrate the truth of such generalizations by repeated descriptions of prosperous merchants, declining landlords, busy towns, and stagnant estates. By controlling the selection of material he was to report upon, by utilizing a number of clever artistic devices to heighten his readers' appreciation of commerce, and by adumbrating the narrative with essays or comments upon his favorite commercial themes, he manages not only to portray the British nation but to picture it as a kind of mercantile utopia.

DEFOE'S USUAL OPINIONS ON BUSINESS

In shifting from the expository mode of his tracts on trade to the narrative form of the *Tour*, Defoe is able to handle his favorite themes differently; rather than hammering away at a particular topic through successive paragraphs, he tends to display his attitudes in scattered references to the various conditions he encounters on his travels. Most often these references are short comments rather than extended essays, and as such they are less fatiguing to the reader than the lengthy passages in his other tracts. His remarks on the direct relationship of populousness to trade make a fair example. He speaks of Chichester as being "not a place of much trade, nor is it very populous" (*Tour*, I. 135), and he asks of Halifax, "If they were so populous at that time [Queen Elizabeth's reign], how must they have increased since? and especially since the late revolution, the trade having been prodigiously encouraged by the great demand of their kersies..." (II. 198). The occasional exception to this rule is also worthy of note: Beverley "is a large and populous town, though I find no considerable manufacture carried on there" (II. 236). A partial answer to this contradiction is the happy circumstance that "the inhabitants of Beverley pay no toll or custom in any port or town in England; to which immunity (I suppose) they owe in great measure, their riches and flourishing condition" (II. 237).

While it is not surprising to find Defoe expressing in the *Tour* attitudes toward trade and manufacturing similar to those in his other commercial works, it is interesting to note that the *Tour* is no more concerned with presenting detailed descriptions of commercial practices or manufacturing techniques than are such admittedly general works as the *Plan* and *Review*. One searches in vain for descriptions of industrial processes such as one finds in eighteenth-century georgic verse: here are no elaborations of the methods by which cloth is woven, coal mined, or steel manufactured. Rogers, who effectively links the *Tour* with the agrarian themes of Virgil's *Georgics*, makes no attempt to relate Defoe to the eighteenth-century georgic tradition of describing agricultural or industrial techniques.[6] The *Tour* is more a catalogue of the various trades and industries of England than an investigation into the methods by which they are conducted.

Defoe mentions "three or four especial manufactures carried on [in Worcestershire], which are peculiar to itself" (II. 46), but he proceeds merely to list them (Monmouth caps, Birmingham iron goods, fine stone pots, lindsey woolseys), not to elaborate upon their manufacture or design; then, having completed his list, he writes, "From Worcester I took a tour into Wales..." (II. 47). At Newcastle he provides not an explanation of how coal is mined but an exclamation on the vastness of the coalpits to be found there; at Manchester, he lauds its trade but does not stop to describe it. (II. 261-66). It is precisely this lack of detail on business operations which lends an air of sameness, of repetitiveness, not only to the volumes of Defoe's *Tour* but to virtually all of his major works on trade, with the obvious exceptions of the *Essay upon Projects* and portions of *The Complete English Tradesman*. He is chiefly concerned to generalize on the importance and extent of business activity, and thus similar generalizations appear throughout all his commercial writings.

In the *Tour*, as in his other commercial works, Defoe only rarely mentions his belief that God has business under his especial protection, but on these rare occasions, he insists upon it emphatically. On his approach to Halifax, he describes

> a situation which I never saw the like of in any part of England; and, I believe, is not to be seen so contrived in any part of the world; I mean coals and running water upon the tops of the highest hills: This seems to have been directed by the wise hand of Providence for the very purpose which is now served by it, namely, the manufactures, which otherwise could not be carried on. (II. 194)

In Scotland, however, he finds a situation which seems to threaten his formulation of God's special interest in business: "though this country of Galloway may be the poorest and empty of commerce, it is, perhaps, the most religious part of all Scotland. Some people, I know, will not think that an equivalent for their poverty" (II. 325). He is quick to assert, nevertheless, that their religion would survive an increase in their standard of living:

> It must be acknowledged, and there my opinion concurs, they might be as religious and as serious as they are; and the more so, the better, and yet, they might at the same time be industrious, and apply themselves to trade, and to reap the advantages nature offers them. (I. 66)

In fact, the example of Yarmouth, a "beautiful town" which is "very rich and increasing in wealth and trade" serves to prove his point: "It is also a very well governed town; and I have nowhere in England observed the Sabbath-Day so exactly kept, or the breach so continually punished as in this place, which I name to their honour" (I. 69). Similarly, at Sturbridge Fair, despite the throngs which attend there, "the fair is like a well fortified city, and there is the least disorder and confusion (I believe) that can be seen anywhere, with so great a concourse of people" (I. 85).

At Yarmouth as elsewhere, Defoe is quick to demonstrate the connection between business and virtue, and, happily, virtue is not its only reward:

> Among all these regularities, it is no wonder if we do not find abundance of revelling... and yet I do not see that the ladies here come behind any of the neighboring countries, either in beauty, breeding, or behavior; to which may be added too, not at all to their disadvantage, that they generally go beyond them in fortunes. (I. 69)

In the *Tour* as well as in his other commercial works, Defoe expends a good deal of effort celebrating the virtue of diligence. He continually asserts the virtuousness of the industrious inhabitants of commercial towns, while he regularly denigrates the idleness and "gayety" of resorts such as Bath:

> There remains little to add, but what relates to the modern customs, the gallantry and diversions of that place, in which I shall be very short; the best part being but a barren subject, and the worst part meriting a satyr, rather than a description. (II. 34)

In a similar fashion, "those people who have nothing to do anywhere else, seem to be the only people who have anything to do at Tunbridge" (I. 126).

On the other hand, note his satisfaction on entering Norfolk ("When we come to Norfolk, we see a face of diligence spread over the whole country" [I. 61]) or Burstall ("A noble scene of industry and application is spread before you here" [II. 203-04]). Halifax, another of Defoe's favorite places, he is pleased to find

> infinitely full of people; those people all full of business; not a beggar, not an idle person to be seen... for it is observable, that the people here, however labourious, generally live to a great age, a certain testimony to the goodness and wholesomeness of the country, which is, without doubt, as healthy as any part of England; nor is the health of the people lessened, but helped and established by their being so constantly employed, and as we call it, their working hard; so that they find a double advantage by their being always in business. (II. 193)

Perhaps his satisfaction is greatest at "several good market towns" near Norwich where the pheasants are so plentiful as to give testimony "that the county had more tradesmen than gentlemen in it"; furthermore, "we saw no idle hands here, but every man busy on the main affair of life, that is to say, getting money" (I. 72).

Another of Defoe's claims for commerce in his tracts on trade is that it acts as a civilizing force, and in the *Tour* he is able to illustrate this contention. One basic means by which commerce acts as a civilizing agent is by merely supplying the wherewithal to alleviate squalor, that is, to provide the physical setting requisite to a well-ordered urban society:

> In a word, there is no town in England, London excepted, that can equal Liverpool for the fineness of the streets, and beauty of the building; many of the houses are all of free stone, and compleatly finished; and all the rest (of the new part I mean) of brick, as handsomely built as London itself.
> (II. 259)

Even more important is the attitude toward one's fellows inculcated by trade; Defoe at times equates this attitude with the spirit of civilization itself:

> We found the people of this country [Glamorganshire] more civilized and more courteous, than in the more mountainous parts [of Wales], where the disposition of the inhabitants seems to be rough, like the country; but here as they seem to converse with the rest of the world, by their commerce, so they are more conversible than their neighbors. (II. 57)

Commerce is the soul of civilization for Defoe, but in the *Tour* he can make his point without resorting to the histrionics of the *Review*.

Similarly, he is able to stress the greatness of England without either becoming heated in the process or needing to provide proofs for his assertions. The *Tour* is an extraordinarily patriotic work; Defoe may not have approved of all of what he actually saw on his travels, but he waxes enthusiastic over the great bulk of what he reports. England's commerce, her people, her system of government — all are the best in the world. "Certain it is," he writes, that "the dexterity of the English sailors in those things [outfitting their ships] is not to be matched by the world" (I. 108). On a more exalted note, England is "a nation who have the greatest privileges, and enjoy the most liberty of any people in the world" (II. 137). At times he makes his claims more pointedly, yet still without advancing proofs:

> If you would expect me to give an account of the city of Hamburg or Danzig or Rotterdam, or any of the second rate cities abroad, which are famed for their commerce, the town of Hull may be a specimen. The place is indeed not so large as those; but in proportion more business done in Hull than in any town of its bigness in Europe. (II. 242)

It is not difficult to prove that Defoe's *Tour* expounds the same attitudes toward business which are to be found in his other commercial works; examples such as these might be multiplied endlessly. More important is an examination of the methods by which Defoe expresses these identical beliefs in the *Tour* but manages to create a more successful impression of the value of commerce. The chief factor in his success is his use of the travel narrative itself, a form which allows him to select what material is convenient for his purposes and to comment upon it in a measured and leisurely fashion. Since his book is a traveler's journal, not a discourse on trade, he is not expected to prove anything. By adopting the persona of a gentleman on a series of journeys, he further gives the impression that his interests are those of many another gentleman as well.

ARTISTIC DEVICES IN THE *TOUR*

For some years there was a minor controversy over whether another eighteenth-century travel account, Johnson's *Journey to the Western Islands of Scotland*, should be considered a work of art or should be automatically denied that distinction because it is a non-fiction travel journal. How one answers this question depends mainly upon one's own subjective definition of what constitutes a work of art.[7]

Because it is immaterial to our present purposes whether Defoe's *Tour* be considered a true work of art, that question is better reserved for discussion by other scholars at another time. Few will deny, however, that the author of a travel account might make use of artistic devices for embellishing his meaning or pointing his moral. Defoe uses a number of such devices in order to exploit the advantage he already has gained over less artful prose by the use of his gentlemanly persona and traveler's format. One of the more fundamental of these devices is the way in which he chooses to structure his book. Rather than making the *Tour* one continuous journey, he breaks it into several circuits, many beginning or ending in London, and each described in a "letter." Besides being a handy presentation for the serialized form in which he published the *Tour*, Defoe is able by these means to stress implicitly the centrality of

London, which is one of the major themes of the work. He shows London to be a vast metropolis with virtually the whole of England serving as its hinterland. Throughout his travels he consistently notes the fact that each English county produces some particular commodity with which it supplies London — salt, cattle, geese, hops, woolens, coal, or whatever.

On several occasions he mentions "that I shall observe how London is in general supplied with all its provisions from the whole body of the nation, and how every part of the island is engaged in some degree or other of that supply" (I. 59) and that "I shall still touch that point, how all the counties of England contribute something toward the subsistence of the great city of London" (I. 55). To show that he makes good on this promise, we need only note his comments that "the whole city of London is chiefly supplied with oysters from this part of the Thames [Milton]" (I. 123), that "an infinite number of large sheep are fed every year and sent up to London market" from Rumney Marsh (I. 125), or that "The market at Darking... from whence this great city of London, and all the dainty doings, which are to be seen there, as to eating, is supplied with provisions" (I. 153). Such patter as this bulks large in the *Tour*, and it is worthy of note not only as evidence of the stress Defoe lays upon the economic centrality of London but also as yet another reminder of the economic vastness of England — London alone requires an *infinite* number of sheep and a *multitude* of fishing-boats; it is this fascination with the large scale of economic activity which exhilarated Defoe as it has animated Chamber of Commerce rhetoric for generations. Notice as well Defoe's Chamber of Commerce-like attachment to his native city: London is less often merely London than it is the *great* city of London. At times he addresses this theme more directly, as from Clapham

> looking north, behold, to crown all, a fair prospect of the whole city of London itself; the most glorious sight without exception, that the whole world at present can show, or perhaps ever could show since the sacking of Rome in the European, and the burning the Temple of Jerusalem in the Asian part of the world. (I. 168)

London, then, is somehow the modern counterpart of the great cities of ancient times. This leads us to observe another of Defoe's artistic devices, his juxtaposition of culture with commerce. London's commerce makes her great, so Defoe seems to say, and her greatness allies her with the great centers of Western tradition. Throughout the *Tour* Defoe periodically interjects accounts of historical figures and events among his descriptions of various economic conditions, with the effect of portraying England's contemporary commercial state as a natural outgrowth of its history. His referring to the corn-market at St. Albans, his sandwiching a reference to the Battle of Hastings between a statement of the dangers which affect merchant shipping and an account of the way local sheep are fattened for the London market, or his making similar insertions concerning Julius Caesar, Thomas Becket, or the mother of Henry VII serve to place business activity within the broad traditions of British life and history.[8]

Defoe also introduces references from English literature on occasion, to much the same effect as his historical interpolations. His treatment of Stratford will serve as an example:

> At this last town, going into the parish church, we saw the monument of old Shakespeare, the famous poet, and whose dramatic performances so justly maintain his character among the British poets; and perhaps will do so to the end of time. The bust of his head is in the wall of the northside of the church, and a flat grave-stone covers the body in the aisle just under him. On which grave-stone these lines are written:
>
> > Good friend, for Jesus's sake, forbear
> > To move the dust that resteth here.
> > Blest be the man that spares these stones,
> > and curst be he, that moves my bones.
>
> The navigation of this river Avon is an exceeding advantage to all this part of the country and also to the commerce of the city of Bristol. For by this river they drive a very great trade for sugar, oil, wine, tobacco, lead...
>
> (III. 42)

Often his literary references are more casual: "upon viewing the beautiful prospect of the river... I could not but call to mind those two excellent lines of Sir John Denham, in his poem, called *Cooper Hill*, viz.

> Tho' deep, yet clear, tho' gentle, yet not dull,
> Strong without rage, without o'erflowing full." (I. 143-44)

Such references as these also lend credence to Defoe's persona of the gentleman-traveler. Other allusions to folk literature are more explicitly concerned with demonstrating the interconnections between British history and commerce; at Maidstone, for example,

> Here likewise, and in the country-adjacent, are great quantities of hops planted, and this is called the Mother of Hop Grounds in England... These were the hops I suppose which were planted at the beginning of the Reformation, and which gave occasion to that old distich:
> > Hops, Reformation, bays, and beer,
> > Came into England all in a year. (I. 113)

Defoe's method of intertwining his descriptions of England's commerce and industry with references to her social and political life may be clearly seen in his description of Newcastle, which he prefaces with an anecdote on nearby Lumley Castle:

> They tell us, that King James the First lodged in this castle at his entrance into England to take possession of the crown, and seeing a fine picture of the ancient pedigree of the family, which carried it very far beyond what his majesty thought credible, turned this good jest upon it to the Bishop of Durham, who showed it him, viz. That indeed he did not know that Adam's name was Lumley before. (II. 250)

From this gentle thrust at aristocracy, he proceeds to describe the populous industrial city of Newcastle: its architecture, including its bridges, wharfs, exchange, and a hospital built by a friendly society; its situation (too smoky for comfort); its industries (coal-mining, glass-making, salt-refining, salmon-picking, ship-building, and iron-working); and its merchants, who "carry on a foreign trade to diverse parts of the world" (II. 252). He then concludes his discussion with some remarks on the defeat of Charles I by the Scots at nearby Hexham and comments that

> I was tempted greatly here to trace the famous Picts Wall, built by the Romans, or rather rebuilt by them from hence to Carlisle... But antiquity not being my business in the work, I omitted the journey, and went on for the north. (II. 252)

It is the commerce and industry of Newcastle which chiefly interest Defoe, yet he gives enough attention to the wider social and political history of the area to demonstrate a kind of harmony between smoky, industrial Newcastle and its storied environs, which include Lumley Castle, the battlefield at Hexham, and the Picts Wall. Defoe's juxtapositions of this sort emphasize the factual point that Newcastle's industry is physically adjacent to its historically important neighborhood and create the artistic impression that Newcastle is perfectly congruent with its surroundings. These surroundings provide a link with the past, but it is Newcastle's manufacturing and trade which hold out its hope for the future.

Although Defoe continually interjects historical material into his narrative, he usually keeps such references brief, and he frequently accompanies them with a disclaimer of any intention to treat historical matters or the rarities of antiquity. He maintains that "My business is rather to give a true and impartial description of the place; a view of the country, its present state as to fertility, commerce, manufacture, and product; with the manners and usages of the people" (II. 137). (This "true and impartial description" is also well characterized by Rogers, who points to "the picture of a thriving, improving, developing society which [Defoe] is concerned to paint throughout the book.[9]) Restatements of this intention crop up repeatedly throughout the *Tour*: "the antiquities, and histories of particular places is not my business here, so much as the present state of them" (I. 156); "I am making modern observations, not writing history" (I. 78); "antiquities as I have observed, not being my province in this work, but a description of things in their present state" (II. 2).

This intermittent *occupatio* serves to stress the point, which is quite evident even without being explicitly announced, that the *Tour* is predominantly concerned with contemporary economic conditions, which Defoe labels "the present state of things." It also serves to point out that, without denigrating historical matters (Defoe seems to omit them reluctantly, as in the example of the Picts Wall), he presents the present state of England "as to fertility, commerce, manufacture and product" as a matter of greater importance than its antiquities. Defoe even manages to drape the *Tour* in the cloak of novelty; all this emphasis upon his travel account being up to date, added to his frequent avoidance of historical material on the grounds that Camden or his "reverend continuator" had already described it, give the impression that Defoe is writing in the very newest mode.

He strengthens this impression of being absolutely up-to-the-minute by regularly deriding virtually all of the various folk traditions and stories that he meets in his travels. Such statements as these assure the readers of the *Tour* that its narrator has a thoroughly modern outlook and is totally out of sympathy with unscientific and superstitious folktales:

> As to the Hell Kettles, so much talked up for a wonder, which are to be seen as we ride from the Tees to Darlington, I had already seen so little of wonder in such country tales, that I was not hastily deluded again. 'Tis evident, they are nothing but old coal pits filled with water by the River Tees. (II. 248)

> The cape or head land of St. Bees, still preserves its name; as for the lady, like that of St. Tabbs beyond Berwick, the story is become fabulous, viz. about her procuring, by her prayers, a deep snow on Midsummer Day, her taming a wild bull that did great damage in the country; these and the like tales, I leave where I found them, (viz.) among the rubbish of the old women and the Romish priests. (II. 273)

Several of Defoe's artistic devices in the *Tour*, then, involve controlling his reader's historical perspective. He points out some lingering superstitions which should be denied, but he presents contemporary business life as being no unwholesome departure from England's traditions; he emphasizes by precept and example the importance of the commercial present.

Most of the other artistic devices which Defoe uses to elevate trade in the *Tour* concern not structure or historical perspective but tone: his use of humor and his relative lack of political polemic create a pleasant aura which improve the reception of his use of the language of trade, his perhaps flattering assumption of their knowledge of business, and his general economic outlook. A number of the humorous passages are concerned with religion and achieve their humor by means of a sectarian jibe; yet most of these are not *violently* sectarian. He describes

> Harrow, a little town on a very high hill, and is therefore called Harrow on the Hill: The church of this town standing upon the summit of the hill, and having a very handsome and high spire, they tell us, King Charles II ridiculing the warm disputes among some critical spiritualists of those time, concerning the visible church of Christ upon earth; used to say of it, that if there was ever a visible church upon earth, he believed this was one.
>
> (II. 14)

He also relates "The famous story of John of Beverly":

> one John, Archbishop of York, a learned and devout man, out of mere pious zeal for religion, and contempt of the world, quitted or renounced his honours and superiority in the Church, and, laying aside the pall, and the mitre, retired to Beverley, and lived here all the rest of his time a recluse.
>
> This story will prompt you to enquire how long ago 'twas, for you know as well as I, and will naturally observe, that very few such bishops are to be found now; it was indeed a long time ago, for it is this very year just five year above a thousand year ago that this happened; for the good man died Anno. Dom. 721. (II. 236)

Other anecdotes, such as that of a custom at Lee's Priory in Essex, are free of controversy: since the time of Henry III, a flitch of bacon was to be awarded to "whatever married man did not repent of his being married, or quarrel, or differ and dispute with his wife, within a year and a day after his marriage, and would swear to the truth of it" (I. 37). Of course, no one had ever qualified for the prize.

Defoe's anti-Catholic bias is quite apparent from time to time, particularly when he encounters legends of local saints, as in the St. Bees example above or in his mention of "this mock saint Thomas Becket" and his shrine, which was "the greatest idol of the world" (I. 117). In treating secular political matters, however, Defoe usually steers clear of controversy; even on the question of Union he maintains a relaxed demeanor. While he is emphatic in stating Glasgow's benefits ("tho' when the Union was making, the rabble of Glasgow made the most formidable attempt to prevent it, yet, now they know better, for they have the greatest addition to trade by it imaginable" [II. 335]), he admits that Edinburgh has not increased its prosperity (one might have expected to see "the trade having flourished, as was reasonably expected upon the Union," yet there is "reason to doubt that this is not the case" [II. 301]). Typical of his treatment of politics is this type of neutral comment:

> I have not concerned this work at all in the debate among us in England, as to Whig and Tory. But I must observe of this town, that, except a few Quakers, they boasted that they had not one Dissenter here, and yet at the same time not one Tory, which is what, I believe, cannot be said of any other town in Great Britain. (II. 247)

Perhaps when Defoe was writing the *Tour* he was ready for a holiday from the incessant political wrangling of his unorthodox journalistic labors.

Defoe's use of language continually favors trade in such casual references as "an eminent weaver of Norwich" (I. 61), "This town is famed for dying" (II. 208), "the greatest fair in England" (I. 153), and "a very noble building here, called the Exchange" (II. 250). In addition, by use of such expressions as "The Manchester trade we all know" (II. 251), he instills the feeling that one *ought* to know the myriad commercial details he discusses. Defoe further strengthens his expression of the centrality of commerce by his method of presentation, for he may be said to write in the language of trade. He relies heavily on figures and statistics in his descriptions and finds importance in mentioning prices, estimates of agricultural and industrial production, distances, acreages, and the extent of new building. His descriptions are fundamentally those of a real estate agent. He mentions rents, values estates, and points out their beauties and defects with an eye to appraisal; whether at Oxford, where he equates the progress of education with the rapidity of new construction, at Blenheim, where he comments on the expense associated with its upkeep, or at Whitehall, where he gives a detailed estimate and specifications for a new palace, Defoe shows his interest to be in market values and the salability of property.

THE IDEAL MERCHANT OBSERVED

While Defoe's various artistic devices — juxtaposing commercial matters with England's historical and cultural heritage, his writing in the language of trade, and his assuming a persona which is at once gentlemanly, unsuperstitious, largely uncontroversial, and appreciative of business — embellish his portrait of commercial England in the *Tour*, the main thrust of the work depends upon the material he selects and upon which he comments. This material is predominantly economic, of course, but it includes information on the social mobility of successful merchants. G. D. H. Cole has identified the nature of Defoe's interests in the *Tour*:

> He looked at England with the eye of a tradesman, appraising most things in the light of their contribution to the economics of the national life, and most people in accordance with their place in the economic rather than the social system. A gentleman's house interested him most when it was occupied by an upstart merchant or financier, a nobleman when he had married into trade. (*Tour*, I. ix)

Further, as Alistair Duckworth points out, "Despite its general lack of party bias, the *Tour* is notable for its virtual eclipse of the England of Tory squires and parsons in favor of that of the Whig grandees and their trading allies."[10] It is evident that by choosing this emphasis rather than serving up the normal tourist fare of cathedrals, ruins, and noble estates, Defoe was presenting his own refraction of British life.

In addition to expressing his opinions and selecting his material in the *Tour*, he also displays his ideals. Nowhere is this more clearly seen than in his introduction of the notion of the ideal merchant. Shinagel points out that Defoe never portrays tradesmen as being dishonest or imprudent in his novels; he cites Defoe's treatment of the "Citizen of London" in *Captain Singleton* as an example of the "'gentleman-trader' ideal," and he maintains that "Defoe is here not so much portraying a person as an ideal."[11] Defoe takes much the same course in the *Tour*. He does occasionally lament the existence of stock-jobbers, regretting the effects of their mischief, particularly in connection with the South-Sea episode, rather than castigating them *à la Review*. Otherwise, the merchant-ideal looms large in the *Tour*. We have only to look at his discussion of Hull, where he maintains: "nor have the merchants of any port in Britain a fairer credit, or fairer character, than the merchants of Hull, as well for the justice of their dealings as the greatness of their substance or funds for trade" (II. 243). Having said this much, it is in keeping that he give the history of a glorious merchant of a former day:

> The story of this de la Pole may not be unwelcome, because, though it be a piece of antiquity, 'tis a piece of honour both to the merchants of Hull, and to the town it self. Sir Michael de la Pole was a merchant of Hull, but first at a place called Raven's Rood in Brabant, where, growing rich, he advanced to King Richard II several thousand pounds in gold for his urgent occasions in his wars; upon which the king invited him to come and live in England, which he did; here the king knighted him, made his son, Michael de la Pole, Earl of Suffolk, and gave him several Lordships in Holderness; and Mr. Camden observes, he is styled by the king in those grants, William de la Pole, Dilectus Valectus & Mercator Noster, so that he was called the King's Merchant. (II. 245)

De la Pole is the very picture of the ideal merchant—rich, respected, titled, and recognized as a true defender of the realm. Defoe's notion of the gentleman-trader can be seen continually forming the basis for his descriptions of the merchants he chooses to comment upon in the *Tour*, and these descriptions form one of the major themes of the work.

COMMERCE AND SURVIVAL

Indeed, four complementary themes—rising merchants and bustling commercial towns, declining noblemen and decaying non-mercantile towns—bulk large in the *Tour*. Speaking of London, Defoe asks

> what must be the immense wealth of the city itself, where such a produce is brought forth? where such prodigious estates are raised in one man's age; instances of which we have seen in those of Sir Josiah Child, Sir John Lethulier, Sir James Bateman, Sir Robert Clayton, Sir William Scawen, and hundreds more; whose beginnings were small, or small compared, and who have exceeded even the greatest part of the nobility of England in Wealth, at their death, and all of their own getting. (I. 169)

These men are all merchants, men of wealth, and possessors of titles. In the course of the *Tour* Defoe approvingly records the existence of the landed estates of merchants, but those of titled merchants he mentions with a kind of reverence which is undoubtedly in keeping with his own emotions on approaching these shrines to the Puritan ethic. Child's far-flung estates give frequent occasion in the Tour for comments on the beauty of his grounds, the security of his dependents, and the mercantile source of his fortune. Similarly, "at LVSVM, Sir John Lethulier, a Turkey merchant lived for many years"; to his sons "he has left plentiful estates in this country, but especially in Essex, where his eldest son has a very noble seat, and estate near Barking" (I. 100). Defoe goes into some detail describing "a most delicious house, built *a la moderne*, as the French call it, by the late Mr. Guy, who was for many years Secretary of the Treasury"; furthermore, "King William did Mr. Guy the honour to dine at this house," and although his Majesty was in hurry, "yet he would not go away without taking a look at the fine gardens." Having established the credentials of the place, Defoe concludes his discussion of it by noting that "This house was afterwards bought by Sir William Gore, a merchant of London" (II. 15).

Descriptions such as these abound in the *Tour*, but as Defoe was fond of warning in *The Complete English Tradesman*, a merchant-financier can never be secure in his new country-house until he leaves off trading:

> The other house is that of Sir John Fellows, late sub-governor of the South-Sea Company, who having the misfortune to fall in the general calamity of the late directors, lost all his unhappy wealth, which he had gained in the company, and a good honestly gotten estate of his own in the bargain.
> (*Tour*, I. 159)

Here Defoe displays his usual distaste for the South-Sea venture and is less sympathetic to its victim than one might expect; yet in other cases he treats the broken merchant with respect. He mentions a hospital "built by Sir John Morden a Turkey merchant of London," whose design

> was to make apartments for forty decayed merchants, to whom he resolved to allow 40 l. per annum, each; with coals, a gown, (and servants to look after their apartments) and many other conveniences so as to make their lives as comfortable as possible, and that, as they had lived like gentlemen, they might die so. (I. 96)

With all due respect to ruined merchants, however, Defoe is naturally more interested in success stories of the Horatio Alger variety, such as that of Lord Viscount Barrington, who was "not born to the title, or estate, or name which he now possesses... His name was Shute, his uncle a linen draper in London... He changed the name of Shute, for that of Barrington, by an act of Parliament." Defoe dutifully records the fact that "His lordship is a Dissenter, and seems to love retirement" and takes this occasion "to observe how the present increase of wealth in the city of London, spreads itself into the country, and plants families and fortunes, who in another age will equal the families of the ancient gentry, who were perhaps bought out" (I. 15). Successful merchants, it seems, are not merely being absorbed into the gentry but are *displacing* them. Traveling through Essex, for instance, on leaving Saffron Walden, "I saw the ruins of the once largest and most magnificent pile in all this part of England, viz. Audley End; built by, and decaying with the noble Dukes and Earls of Suffolk." The next town is Braintree: "the manour of Braintree I found descended by purchase, to the name of Olmeus, the son of a London merchant of the same name; making good what I had observed before, of the great number of such who have purchased estates in this country" (I. 88). The juxtaposition of the two case histories serves to highlight the rise of the merchant class at the expense of the current gentry and nobility, and it also underscores Defoe's obviously conscious intention ("making good what I had observed before") of illustrating the social importance of the more successful merchants.

Old families which are straitened need not decline. They may even improve their holdings by the timeless aristocratic ploy of marrying the new wealth, as Defoe shows in this example:

> here is a fine dwelling the ancient seat of the Cordells, whereof Sir William Cordell was Master of the Rolls in the time of Queen Elizabeth; but the family is now extinct; the last heir, Sir John Cordell, being killed by a fall from his horse, died unmarried, leaving three sisters co-heiresses to a very noble estate most of which, if not all, is now centered in the only surviving sister, and with her in marriage is given to Mr. Firebrass, eldest son of Sir Basil Firebrass, formerly a flourishing merchant in London.   (I. 48-49)

On the other hand, Defoe does meet some people who "have no notion of being rich and populous, and thriving by commerce" (II. 324); in southwestern Scotland he even records the incomprehensible attitudes of

> the gentry [who] have no genius to trade; 'tis a mechanism which they scorn; though their estates are not able to feed them, they will not turn their hands to business or improvement; they had rather see their sons made foot soldiers, (than which, as officers treat them now, there is not a more abject thing on earth), than see them apply to trade, nay, to merchandise, or to the sea, because those things are not (forsooth) fit for gentlemen.   (II. 76)

Although Defoe is quick to record the rise of a merchant or the decay of county family, he conducts no campaign of shrill invective against the gentry in the *Tour*, and this fact alone goes a long way toward making it a more effective encomium of business than is his *Review*. He often notes in the *Tour* that "the country is, as it were, covered with fine palaces of the nobility, and pleasant seats of the gentlemen" (I. 134) or that "These and a great many more ['fine seats of the nobility and gentlemen'] lying so near together, make the country hereabout much more sociable and pleasant" (II. 133); such comments as these also help him to maintain his persona of a traveling gentleman.

Nevertheless, other than in the cases of intermarriage between city and county families or the acquisition of country estates by merchants, he usually perceives merchants and gentlemen to be inhabiting different worlds: "here [at Maidstone] is, what is not often found, namely, a town of very great business and trade, and yet full of gentry, of mirth, and of good company" (I. 115). As in *The Complete English Tradesman*, Defoe maintains that being either a merchant or a country gentleman is a fulltime job and that on changing stations, one must adopt new habits. Just as Defoe frequently makes mention of rising merchants and declining gentry, he continually notes the existence of towns which thrive by commerce and those which decay through neglect of it. He is pleased to find in one county "three towns [Norwich, Yarmouth, and Lynn] so populous, so rich, and so famous for trade and navigation" (I. 62). Norwich, indeed, is the "capitol of all the county and the center of all the trade and manufactures.... an ancient, large, rich, and populous city ... Nor does it seem to be, like some ancient places, a decayed declining town" (I. 63). To find an exception to his rule that commercial towns are prosperous and growing towns is a mystifying experience: "But for a private town, a sea-port, and a town of commerce, to decay, as it were of itself (for we never read of Dunwich being plundered or ruined by any disaster, at least not of late years); this I must confess, seems owing to nothing but the fate of things..." (I. 54).

The fate of non-commercial towns is more sure. Of Launceston Defoe says, "As to trade, it is not much to boast of," which comes as no surprise, for he has already described it as "showing little else, but marks of its antiquity...an old, ragged, decayed place, in general" (I. 258, 257). He continually identifies trade with modernity and "antiquity" with stagnation, as in his description of Lancaster:

> The town is ancient; it lies, as it were, in its own ruins, and has little to recommend it but a decayed castle and a more decayed port (for no ships of any considerable burden); the bridge is handsome and strong, but, as before, here is little or no trade, and few people. (II. 268)

Lack of trade may be the main cause of municipal decline, but an excess of competition can also have adverse effects, as at Ipswich: "the neighborhood of London, which sucks the vitals of trade in this island to itself, is the chief reason of any decay of business in this place" (I. 43).

DEFOE'S SUBJECTIVITY

Defoe's predominantly economic world view, as it is reflected in the *Tour*, portrays merchants and trading centers as the active, creative forces in the culture and pictures the gentry and town which neglect business as pockets of social stagnation. Defoe's view, however, was hardly the universally accepted impression of his day. Consider these descriptions of the same town:

> As to Leicester, accounted 12 miles from Harborough, it is now an old stinking town, situated upon a dull river, inhabited for the most part by tradesmen, viz: worsted combers and clothiers, for the streets being then a sweeping and cleansing against the judges coming in the next morning the stinking puddles of and water being then stirred, made me go spewing all through the streets as I went to see it, yet it hath formerly been a town of good remark, for here is an ancient house or palace called the Duke of Lancaster's palace, as also a large hospital built by some of those dukes, and an old piece of building which they call Janus' temple. (Thomas Baskerville, 1630-1720)[12]

> Leicester is an ancient large and populous town, containing about about five parishes, 'tis the capital of the county of Leicester, and stands on the River Soar, which rises not far from that High Cross I mentioned before: They have a considerable manufacture carried on here, and in several of the market towns round for weaving of stockings by frames; and one would scarce think it possible so small an article of trade could employ such multitudes of people as it does; for the whole county seems to be employed in it.... (Defoe, *Tour*, II. 88-89)

To Baskerville, Leicester is a disgusting remnant of its former aristocratic glory; for Defoe, it is an inspiring sight of energy and industry.

Nor could we ever confuse the feelings of Defoe, the Dissenter, admirer of merchants, and tool of the first Earl of Oxford, with the sentiments of the second Earl's chaplain, who, while attending his lordship on his travels, thus describes a particularly ostentatious memorial:

> The person who ordered this splendid monument and the other marble one in the church was one Isles, who was a poor lad of the poorer rank of this town, and had been bound to some inferior trade in it,' but run away from his master to London, where he got into some way of life which enabled him to leave this memorandum of himself and his family. Our landlord informed us (which I could hardly believe, considering his zeal for a remembrance both in the inside and the outside of the church) that Isles was a Dissenter and a Presbyterian; but when I recollected, my knowledge and acquaintance with some of those people, I could easily reconcile it.[13]

This display calls to mind nothing so much as Defoe's diametrically opposite opinion of another socially-mobile individual, Viscount Barrington: "His lordship is a Dissenter, and seems to love retirement" (*Tour*, I. 15). It is hardly necessary to belabor the point that Defoe's description of England in the *Tour* is a subjective impression rather than a universally-held view; the burgeoning commercial and industrial towns and the growing wealth and prestige of the merchant class were indeed matters of some ambiguity. Defoe looks upon these developments favorably and stresses their economic benefits,· while others who were more attached to the *status quo* might understandably consider them threats to the culture.

While noting this disparity of opinion, and without impugning Defoe's preeminence as a defender of commerce, we must refrain, nevertheless, from conceding him the mantle of uniqueness for his attitudes. There was a goodly amount of interest in and approval of commercial and industrial techniques among Defoe's contemporaries and predecessors. This interest did not really become fashionable in polite literature until the emergence of Thomson and the georgic poets, largely after the publication of the *Tour*, but it had already become a fixture of much travel literature which predated or was contemporary with Defoe's travels. William Stukeley, the antiquary, may provide an unlikely example; his biographer writes concerning the *Itinerarium Curiosum* (1725):

> At Manchester, "the most rich, populous and busy village in *England*," industries and the new church "after the London models" receive comment in a manner as unantiquarian as that of Defoe, though naturally the Roman remains at Chester are noticed.[14]

An earlier and even more enthusiastic example is provided by Celia Fiennes, sister of the Third Viscount of Saye and Sele, author of *Through England on a Sidesaddle in the Time of William and Mary* (not published until 1888), who is mentioned by Trevelyan as being "a lady of means and a Dissenter."[15] Margaret Willy accurately describes the commercial aspects of this journal:

> She had, too, what seems a somewhat unfeminine interest in the different trades and industries of the places she visited. Not content merely to catalogue these, she went wherever she could to watch the work in progress, and set down with painstaking exactitude details of manufacturing processes. We hear of glove-making in Derby and stocking-weaving in Nottingham, and the cloth trade of Colchester, Norwich, and Leeds; of shipbuilding in the

dockyards at Rochester; of the hopfields and cherry orchards of Kent, the cultivation of liquorice in Pontefract, and cider-making in somerset and Herefordshire. Fuller accounts are given of the manufacture of products, from salt in Cheshire to serge in Exeter; of the silk-weaving and paper-making at Canterbury, of the drainage system in the fens, and above all of mining — marble, copper, tin and lead, and coal (of which she favorably compares the price in the midlands with what she has to pay in London).[16]

Defoe's description of England, then, represents his own particular view of British life, but however important this view might be, it should not be considered wholly original with him.

Defoe's real achievement in the *Tour* is in weaving his attitudes toward business and his observations on Britain into a cohesive frame. Perhaps most surprising for a guide book is that the *Tour* has a discernable artistic pattern: it weaves virtually all of his favorite commercial themes — such as the primacy of trade and manufactures, their importance to all classes, their dynamism, and their importance to England — into a celebration of British commercial life. By adopting the format of traveling through the entire country, Defoe is able to make pronouncements on the conduct of business and to sharpen his moral by pointing out, for instance, a decaying town which regulates trade or a house sold at a distressed price by a ruined stock-jobber. His presentation further confirms and reinforces his artistic pattern: his often-stated intention to avoid the usual tourist fare, his choice of subject matter as chiefly descriptions of commercial and manufacturing activities, his digressions on the importance of trade or on more technical business matters, his style of presentation in looking at England through the eyes of a real-estate agent and in valuing the use of figures and statistics, and his general view of society on the theme of the decaying nobility and the rising merchant — all combine to fit England into his own world view.

Defoe's view of society completes his characterization of England as a commercial nation. He fills the *Tour* with references to declining or extinct families of nobility (who have not embraced trade), to the physical decline of church buildings and revenues and to a similar decline of the heavily-regulated corporation towns, and to rising, landed, or titled merchants. His emphasis throughout is on wealth, prosperity, and populousness. He depicts an England which has been lifted out of the Medieval period by the one vital force of business activity. Furthermore, he pictures this force as being fundamentally restorative to British life; he hardly mentions the destructive side of change. In the *Review*, Defoe continually stresses the fact that trade ought to be the prime concern of the nation; in the world which he describes in the *Tour*, trade *is* life's most important concern. Because of his non-argumentative tone, because of his comprehensive view of trade, and because of his convincing yet often subtle presentation of the value of commerce to England, the *Tour* is by far his most effective popularization of business.

CHAPTER IV

Defoe's Business Ethics

Opinions on the general condition of business ethics and on the ethical ramifications of particular business situations are virtually doomed to be unfavorable. This state of affairs would seem due to the morally ambiguous nature of business activity rather than the moral fiber of the men and women who conduct business enterprises. In the first place, as with many other forms of endeavor, there are no uniform standards by which observers judge commercial activity. One observer has described the West's "confused ethical heritage" as being influenced by

- The Hebraic culture, based on the Ten Commandments, with emphasis on the group in total "covenant."
- The Christian system, based on the Beatitudes, with emphasis on the individual born into the Kingdom.
- The Medieval way of life, based on penance, with emphasis on the future life.
- The Renaissance culture, based on the individual and his freedom.
- The Industrial Revolution, based on the technical application of science to production and distribution.
- The scientific approach, based on the empirical method and the reign of law.[1]

Oversimplified and incomplete as this list is, it makes its point, for the potential conflicts between these various legitimate and viable influences are obvious. Valid criticisms based on a number of such standards may thus be directed at any particular action.

There are other problems as well which are fundamental to the practice of business. The potentially conflicting interests of owners, employees, customers, government, the public, and the environment must be reconciled continually. Even more fundamental, however, is the tension between aggressiveness and servility which is at the very heart of capitalistic enterprise. Business is a mechanism through which people serve their own acquisitive instincts by serving the needs of others. There must be a continual search for an optimum between rapacity (such as that of the American railroads of the 1890's) on the one hand, and bankruptcy on the other. Another problem, one that Defoe confronts in his commercial writings, is the responsibility of business to its customers. The degree of responsibility of a seller to prevent the misuse of goods by a buyer, for instance, is hardly any clearer in the twentieth century than in the eighteenth. A final and quite basic problem is that business is essentially an active rather than a contemplative pursuit; business practitioners must be striving constantly to make a living, to make a profit, or to make ends meet. In the process they generate countless actions which may be observed and judged by an audience of associates, competitors, and the public at large; because of this high level of activity they frequently expose themselves to the risk of criticism.

As a result of the moral complexities and ambiguities inherent in business activity, no satisfactory code of business ethics has yet been devised, despite many attempts. A thoroughly representative early essay is Thomas Fuller's "The Good Merchant" (1642). He details seven rules, including "He wrongs not the buyer in number, weight, or measure," "He makes not advantage of his chapman's ignorance," and "Selling by retail he may justify the taking of greater gain." Fuller at last gives up the attempt to set down a comprehensive list of standards, saying

> But how long shall I be retailing our rules to our merchant? It would employ a casuist an apprentice-ship of years: take our Saviour's wholesale rule, *Whatsoever ye would have men do unto you, do you unto them; for this is the Law, and the Prophets.*[2]

A more recent attempt, and one which is hardly more explicit or helpful than Fuller's exposition of the Golden Rule, suggests that

> 1. The professional business manager affirms that he will place the interest of the business for which he works before his own private interests.
> 2. The professional business manager affirms that he will place his duty to society above his duty to his company and above his private interest.[3]

Such platitudinous statements as these provide no more definite guidance to business executives struggling with a complex and immediate decision than do the vaguest of good intentions, yet these prescriptions are among the best essays toward a code of business ethics which four centuries of thought and experience have produced. In attempting to assay the quality of Defoe's ethical habits of mind, then, it is hardly appropriate to apply private or topical standards; nor is it wise, considering the welter of conflicting interests which those engaged in business must regularly attempt to reconcile or pacify, to make blanket condemnations of his attitude toward business decisions on the basis of general precepts such as the Golden Rule, however unassailable such precepts may be.

INADEQUACY OF CRITICISM OF DEFOE'S ETHICS

Traditionally, the thought that has been expended on Defoe's business ethics has been based on general prescriptions and has not reflected much awareness of the complex moral environment in which business operates. Accordingly, and not surprisingly, most such criticism has been inordinately harsh. Certainly we may find some weak reasoning, some obvious contradictions, and some ominous lacunae in Defoe's ethics. Yet previous critics have shown themselves more eager to judge than to analyze, more interested to condemn than to understand. Such treatment is quite understandable in view of the circumstances of Defoe's own career: his perhaps having defrauded his own family, his frequent flights from the law, his residence in prison, his having been exposed in the pillory, and his unsavory journalistic career. Regardless of the fact that today we might think the pillory a cruel and unusual punishment or the debtors' statutes to have been bad laws, during his lifetime Defoe was a fugitive from the law, a convict, and a public reprobate. Such a reputation as this is not likely to inspire confidence in Defoe the moralist.

Paul Dottin's description sums up the traditional attitude toward Defoe's business ethics: "His scrupulosity was based upon the old saying 'The end justifies the means.' Success, interpreted as material gain, was the keynote of his philosophy and, indeed, of his morality."[4] Our most detailed investigations of Defoe's ethical values are those of Hans H. Andersen in 1941 and Denis Donoghue in 1963, and they agree in general with Dottin's assessment.[5] Andersen states of Defoe that "whenever he drew a distinction between economic and ethical ends he did so in defense of economic expediency," that "a mere respectful reference to ethical objections, immediately and openly dismissed from practical consideration, implied at least orthodoxy in the author at the same time that the dismissal saved him the trouble of having to deal with them."[6] He concludes thus:

> The work of Defoe is an intimate revelation of the conflict between morality and commercialism in his age. He did not see the paradox with the complete

intellectual detachment of Mandeville. He looked before and after. But he was consistent with reference to either direction and consistent also, finally, in voicing and supporting to the last the aspirations of England's increasing commerce, though he continued to pay morality the conventional, if economically inexpensive, tributes.[7]

"The bourgeois attainments," agrees Donoghue, "are the only qualities which Defoe admired."[8] Furthermore, "If religion and trade could proceed happily together, like Plato's horses, well and good; but if a dispute arose, religion must yield, we are a trading nation, we must be loyal to our calling. This is the rhetoric of *Mercator* and *Review*."[9] While these statements correctly describe an observable *tendency* in Defoe's work, they can be shown to be inaccurate in the categorical form in which they are presented. Andersen and Donoghue are largely in agreement not only in their general conclusions but in the specific charges they make against Defoe as well. The two issues on which they find Defoe lacking concern are his approval of traffic in slaves and trade in luxuries. Donoghue also becomes exercised over what he considers to be a superficial religious feeling in Defoe. The three charges merit individual discussion.

On the matter of the slave trade, it is quite true that Defoe shows himself to be remarkably and unambiguously in favor of it. In recommending the colonization of Africa, he points to the relative cheapness of the price of slaves there as an economic incentive to establish plantations (*Plan*, p. 250). In the *Essay upon Projects* he suggests the purchase of two hundred slaves ("generally persons that do a great deal of work") to repair the highways (*Essay*, p. 20). Nor is Defoe particularly humane in his attitudes toward the treatment of slaves:

> the Negroes are indeed slaves, and our good people use them like slaves, or rather like dogs, *but that by the way*: he that keeps them in subjection, whips, and corrects them in order, to make them grind and labour, *does right*, for out of their labour he gains his wealth: but he that in his passion and cruelty, maims, lames and kills them, *is a fool*, for they are his estate, his stock, his wealth, and his prosperity. (*Review*, VIII, 730)

Once having discovered that Defoe favored the slave trade, however, what have we proved? Andersen and Donoghue find this a signal of moral laxity; their position is firmly rooted in nineteenth- and twentieth-century attitudes toward Negro slavery. Yet they do not broaden their charge to include such contemporaries of Defoe as the Members of

Parliament who voted to preserve the Africa trade or the Ministers who successfully negotiated for the Asiento.

The point is that while it is socially reprehensible to advocate slavery in the twentieth century, it was socially acceptable to do so in the eighteenth. If George Washington's character, for instance, has not suffered as a result of his having been a slaveowner, it seems strange that Defoe should be attacked for merely writing on the subject. Social acceptance aside, there seems to have been no clear moral agreement on the matter up to Defoe's time. Slaves formed an important part of economic and political life in the West from anitiquity to the nineteenth century. One remembers Pope Gregory the Great's pun on an English slave, likening the blond Angle to an angel, but one sees his energies being poured into converting the English to Christianity rather than into destroying slavery itself. Lately, in fact, a major challenge has even been issued to the older belief that the anti-slavery movement of the nineteenth century was a selfless, noble crusade. Eric Williams maintains that England's abolition of the slave trade was effected not primarily for libertarian reasons but largely in order to protect the British sugar trade with the West Indies and was made possible by the fact that by 1807 the slave trade itself had declined to a rather inconsiderable fraction of total British commerce.[10] From a twentieth-century point of view, Andersen and Donoghue have a socially and morally unassailable case; from an eighteenth-century view, however, Defoe must have seemed an ordinary and even a responsible spokesman. The two periods simply have antithetical opinions on the question, and there the matter must rest.

Were it appropriate to attack Defoe's moral stand on slavery, however, we should not omit to chastise his position on pollution abatement as well. His blindness to this issue is almost total. Speaking of Newcastle, he says merely that "The situation of the town to the landward is exceeding unpleasant... the smoke of the coals, makes it not the pleasantest place in the world to live in" (*Tour*, II. 251). Even worse is this description of Yarmouth:

> The only inconvenience with which this town is reproached, is the smell, which is indeed offensive to strangers, during the fishing fair.... Just so London may be said to stink of smoke, Wapping of tar, Seville of oil, etc. but *lucri dulcis odor*.[11]

Here are no schemes from Defoe the projector to remedy an unpleasant situation. Noxious effluent and emissions were not yet of sufficient concentration in the eighteenth century to spark an ecological outcry such as we have in the twentieth; nor can we imagine a generation which regularly hurled the contents of its chamber-pots into the public streets unduly offended by coal-smoke in Newcastle. Certain issues provoke ethical crises in every age, but slavery and pollution were not so recognized in the early eighteenth century.

The matter of trade in luxuries is more involved and was more frequently discussed in Defoe's day. Donoghue states the dilemma nicely in his comment that "Defoe agreed that luxurious living was wrong, but on the other hand it was the very life of trade."[12] Yet Defoe was not entirely consistent in maintaining that luxurious living was a bad thing. Often he writes as if trading in luxuries is a very serious vice indeed; for example, he exclaims in the *Review* that "Such is the present state of our trade, that we are in debt to the Devil; that whenever we break our confederacy with *Satan* we are certainly ruined and undone" (*Review*, IX. 82). Yet only a few weeks later, he takes a more benign view of luxury goods:

> It is true, the common mercies of life, and such as mankind can least want, our bountiful Creator has made most universal... [but] many of the numberless *addenda* to the pleasures and conveniences of life; nay, some of the most sovereign remedies in capital distempers, how are they fixed in the remotest parts of the world, in the inaccessible caverns of the earth, or beyond the unpassable oceans? When I say, inaccessible and unpassable, I am to be understood, inaccessible and unpassable but by labor, industry, and correspondence, *and this is* TRADE. (*Review*, IX, 110.)

In these and other similar quotations, Defoe thus virtually simultaneously condemns the sale and commends the use of luxuries.

Much of this sort of confusion derives from the nature of the "luxuries" which he discusses and the manner in which he discusses them. Contrast his degree of emphasis in these two passages:

> If necessity is the mother of trade, luxury is as surely the consequence of riches and plenty; and we are certainly arrived to such a pitch in all manner of riot and excess, that we have to apprehend the fatal effects to ourselves, that always have followed from the same causes, in the greatest and most potent empires, as those of Persia, Greece, Rome, etc., which were dissolved by their luxury. (*CET*, II. 230)

> It is next to incredible what a share the luxury of the age has, in the employment of families, and in the multiplying of tradesmen in this nation, among whom, no one article they deal in may be called a necessity to life, or even to the real comforts of it. (*CET*, II. 225-26)

In both of these cases as well as in others where he actually elaborates, Defoe seems to be speaking not of dealers in such dark vices as prostitution or narcotics or gambling. Rather, he scores "the exorbitancies of dress, the excesses of eating and drinking" (*CET*, II. 226), the trades of peruke-makers, pastry cooks, and undertakers (*CET*, II. 232), the vices of "the fop, the beau, the drunkard, the dancing-master" (*Review*, VIII. 739), and the wares of dealers in "baubles and ridiculous knick-knacks" (*Review*, IX. 82), china, chocolate, coffee, and tea — all of which, as well as wine and fashions, Defoe himself had dealt in at various times.

Luxury, of course, is a relative matter; fire and the wheel were doubtless great luxuries when they were first discovered, whereas they have become necessities to later ages. The luxuries which exercised Defoe seem to twentieth-century observers either laughable (perukes) or overplayed (pastries). Certain of his preoccupations (undertakers) have raised a hue and cry in our own century (Jessica Mitford's *The American Way of Death*, for instance), but the persistence of elaborate burial customs from Defoe's time to our own perhaps merely reemphasizes the fact that human behavior expresses needs which mere economic logic cannot explain. Watching Defoe squirm while attempting to rationalize what he considers to be luxury traffic, we witness not so much a conflict between morality and immorality as a clash between two of the radically-opposed tenets of the Puritan ethic: the urge to work and prosper and the need to live abstemiously. Nowhere is this struggle seen more clearly than in a case to which Defoe makes casual reference, that of "those Quakers who deal in finery and ornament, but never wear themselves" (*CET*, II. 230). Setting aside temporarily the issue of morality, this example does point up a notable shortcoming in the business ethics of some Puritan merchants. Whether or not the wearing of such "finery and ornament" be considered sinful, surely it shows a certain lack of ethical delicacy for merchants to handle goods which they themselves feel are unworthy of their own patronage. Such a case as this in which the seller recognizes an absolute prohibition against the commodity is reasonably clear-cut and is qualitatively different from the situation of one who deals in liquor or pharmaceuticals, does not believe his goods to be inherently evil, but does recognize that the misuse or excessive use of the products may be harmful or sinful. Neither Defoe nor Andersen and Donoghue make this distinction.

As we have seen, Defoe shows himself to be uncertain as to the status of luxuries; he assumes luxuries to be an evil but "comforts" to be a blessing, yet he does not define the difference. In addition, the luxuries he does condemn do not pander to man's darkest vices but rather to social indiscretions. Types such as the fop, the beau, the drunkard, the dancing-master — these are subjects fit not for prison but for satire or pity. And while their peccadilloes might be socially undesirable, they do produce compensating social benefits: "it frequently appears that the extravagant pride of the age feeds trade, and, consequently, the poor" (*CET*, II. 231). Again, in a decidedly Mandevillian vein:

> Since then our vices are by necessity thus made virtues in our trade, we must allow those things we call superfluities, to be necessities in trade; and it is manifest, that he would go about to reform effectually, the common vices and luxury of the nation, at the same time begins the ruin of our trade; and by the time he has brought us to be a nation of saints, he will be sure to make us a nation of beggars. (*Review*, VIII. 739)

The choice of words here calls forth a vision of life under the Protectorate, when the attempt to reform "common vices" occasioned a loss of individual liberty. Defoe does not make the argument for liberty part of his defense of luxury trade, however; he is content simply to point out that any but the most rigid customs enforcement would be futile, for pleasureseekers would merely buy luxury goods from abroad if British merchants were forbidden to trade in them. The prospect of the out-flow of gold resulting from such a move would have been enough to make a mercantilist shudder.

Furthermore, anyone familiar with Defoe's thought must immediately sense the paradox in his "nation of saints... nation of beggars." As Maximillian Novak has pointed out, Defoe is remarkably consistent in his attitudes toward those reduced to a state of necessity, even to the point of absolving them of guilt for actions which when committed by less needy persons would be criminal.[13] The declaration "necessity is the parent of crime" and the prayer "give me not poverty lest I steal" occur repeatedly throughout Defoe's works. For these reasons, Defoe would have considered any action which reduced a nation to beggary to be a great evil.

Defoe is similarly consistent in placing the blame for England's luxury traffic not on the tradesman but on the customer:

> the trade does not make the vice, but the vice makes the trade; if the tradesmen propagate crimes in the ordinary way of their business, the fault is not in the trade, but in the man; as in the case of drunkenness, the grape, and the malt, are not chargeable; they are an innocent product....
>
> (*CET*, II. 230)

The tradesman's desire to make a living is an innocent one; further, because Defoe allows that the temptation is not in the luxury goods but in the man himself, then the guilt accrues not to the seller but to the buyer:

> trade, take it in the first person of the tradesman, does not introduce the luxury and extravagance of the people; nor their exorbitant expense in fine clothes, or fine equipages, their pride and ostentation in either or any of these; but the vice is in the breast of the vicious: the pride is in the inside of the beau, while his embroideries, his laces, his fine clothes, only flutter in the wind from the outside of his carcass. (*CET*, II. 230-31)

To Defoe, the evil is in the consumer. Such reasoning as this from *The Complete English Tradesman* is in line with comments in *Moll Flanders* and *The Fortunate Mistress* in which he maintains that the needy prostitute is free of guilt and that her lustful customer is wholly responsible for the sin committed. Such a position is extreme and unorthodox, yet it seems not to have been an argument hastily assembled to defend trade but rather a matter of conviction with Defoe. It is also a position with a strangely modern ring, given twentieth-century "John Laws" which prosecute clients as well as prostitutes.

A final matter worthy of note on Defoe's attitudes toward the luxury trade is that he occasionally did make suggestions for restraining or regulating such traffic, thus quieting the suspicion that he invariably wrote in favor of continuing trade in luxuries. The difficulty with such declarations is that he is hopelessly vague as to the details of the restraint he intends; for instance, he recommends the enactment of "a good sumptuary law" (*CET*, II. 234), but he does not explain how a good law might differ from a bad one. He also maintains that:

> The excursions, the nuisances, the vicious part of this trade may be restrained, and so far as it touches our morals, ought to be restrained; but to bring down all those common excrescences of mode, habit, fashion, and custom in apparel, which are in the general practice of trade, become a very considerable part of the employment of our people, would be to unhinge the whole nation, load every parish and town with starving people, ruined tradesmen, and the rich would hardly be able to support the poor.
>
> (*Review*, III. 66)

The remedy he proposes is to extend no credit for luxuries. This is a rather clever suggestion on Defoe's part, inasmuch as one of the objections to luxuries is that people of various stations may spend on them beyond their means to the detriment of their family and their posterity. Again, however, he does not specify which luxuries are to be affected nor how the law might be enforced. The weakest aspect of Defoe's writings on luxuries is the vagueness and off-handedness of his suggestions for reform.

On the surface, Andersen and Donoghue have a case to make about Defoe's tendency to favor economic over moral considerations in relation to trade in luxuries. His suggestions for reform are indeed a bit half-hearted. And while he carries on excitedly about luxuries ruining our morals, he almost invariably ends by defending the trade. But looking deeper we see that the vices he describes are largely those of overindulgence rather than criminality. Further, while he argues in favor of economic expediency (against reducing tradesmen and laborers to pauperism), we find that his economic arguments are based on his deeply-held convictions of necessity and morality, that to reduce people to beggary is to force them to commit acts such as robbery and murder which society agrees are truly criminal. Even should such prohibitions and their resultant poverty come to pass, however, they would not solve the problem, the vice being in the breast of consumers who would merely obtain luxury goods from abroad. To increase criminality without diminishing the lesser evil of luxurious living, Defoe argues, is not only economically foolish but morally evil. Andersen and Donoghue certainly have a point, but they state their case a bit superficially.

Besides the problem of slavery and luxuries, Donoghue finds Defoe lacking in the quality of his religious feeling. What seems to disturb him is Defoe's commercial imagery: "Defoe assented to Christian ethics only to the extent that it proved amenable to the analogies of trade"; "Defoe spoke a commercial language and was not prepared to change it when the problem of ethical translation became acute"; "Religion is a transaction; God is an excellent trading connection."[14] Donoghue's over-emphasis of Defoe's commercial imagery is unfortunate, for as on the matter of luxuries his article does have a point — Defoe's religious sentiments *are* often phrased in "analogies of trade." But to go on to state that the mere fact of this commercial imagery is itself a sign of a lack of religious feeling undermines confidence in Donoghue's entire essay, which is by no means wholly without merit. He writes, "The significant aspect of his [Crusoe's] thought, however, is that it is conducted entirely through the analogies of trade. He interprets 'Call on me in the day of trouble' as a promissory note: God's Covenant is literally understood as a commercial bargain."[15] Furthermore, "Defoe's attitudes are strictly continuous with Crusoe's."[16]

Since Defoe's religious imagery does not touch directly on the problem of his business ethics, we can afford little space to discuss it here. It is important, however, as an example of the unfortunate way in which Defoe tends to be characterized as a single-dimensioned commercial fanatic who was unique in his age. While Defoe uses a great deal of religious-commercial imagery, a glance into his *Meditations* will show that he is capable of other modes of thought. Secondly, Defoe was hardly alone among his contemporaries in making use of the "analogies of trade"; recall Dryden in *The Hind and the Panther*:

> Faith is the best ensurer of thy bliss;
> The bank above must fail before the venture miss.[17]

Further, it is difficult to see why the agricultural imagery of the New Testament is preferable (other than as a matter of habit, tradition, or taste) to the commercial imagery of the eighteenth century: surely the difference between visualizing one's God as a shepherd rather than as a banker cannot reasonably be thought to affect the quality of the religious feeling involved. Finally, there are some valid analogies between trade and Christianity. To oversimplify hugely, in many Christian systems one's reward (heaven) is based largely on service to others; in business, one's reward (profits) is similarly based on service to one's fellows.

Donoghue goes on to present another stereotyped view in stating that "Defoe's vision of life was a network of analogies drawn from the priority of middle-class trade. This meant that certain qualities and feelings had to be sacrificed to the main commercial chance."[18] Such singleminded dedication to an economic goal is very much unlike Defoe, who left a prospering wholesaling business to join the ranks of the adventurer Monmouth, and who jeopardized his brick factory by writing a poem such as "The Shortest Way with the Dissenters." True, in *The Complete English Tradesman*, Defoe urged businessmen to be more single-minded than he had been, but even twentieth-century studies of this aspect of corporate life show that business executives have a range of interests more similar to Defoe's own than to any unwavering ideal he may be thought to propound.[19] After setting aside the matter of Defoe's own experiences, and even after granting that his recipe for commercial success is a strenuous one, such dedication to trade is only half of his social message in the *Complete English Tradesman* and *Gentleman*; equally important is his repeated assertion that a merchant must *abandon* active participation in commercial enterprises upon achieving his ultimate goal of becoming a gentleman.

DEFOE'S LACK OF FORMAL ETHICAL CODE

Defoe never did formally codify his attitudes on business ethics; these attitudes appear throughout his writings on trade and must be extracted from that mass of literature. So far as his opinions on particular issues are concerned, we have seen that Defoe was merely a child of his own times in relation to such matters as pollution and slavery and that he struggled intensely enough in the *Review* and other tracts with the problem of trade in luxury goods to reach a solution amenable to his own presuppositions on human nature. Some mention should be made as well of his general attitudes toward the moral tenor of business. Defoe frequently mentions his belief in the correlation of industriousness in trade with lawfulness in society. In the *Tour*, for instance, he praises the orderliness of such prime trading areas as Yarmouth and Sturbridge Fair while castigating the deportment of the citizens of Feversham, which has "no particular remarkable trade, either for manufacture or navigation" (*Tour*, I. 111). Michael Shinagel observes Defoe's uniformly favorable portrayal of businessmen in the novels:

> The virtual absence of dishonest or imprudent business transactions in his novels is remarkable. Indeed, the business decorum and skill of the characters, major and minor, is idealized to a fault, as if Defoe were unable to bring himself to portray any improper actions when it came to the transaction of business.[20]

This is to say that the matter of business ethics continually reappears throughout most of his writings on trade and works of fiction. He comes closest to a formal statement on the importance of ethics in trade with his *Complete English Tradesman*, which, as Shinagel reports, "was not only a practical manual on how to succeed in business but also a conduct book designed to dignify the profession and polish the men who practice it."[21] Honesty and fair dealing constitute an important part of the conduct Defoe exalts; he sets up an ideal of the "honest, open-hearted, generous, fair-dealing tradesman," stating

> that everybody speaks well of him, loves to deal with him; and whether they get or lose by him, they are always pleased; that he treats the rich with good manners, and the poor with good language; and that in particular he is a punctual paymaster; that when he has made a bargain, whether he gets or loses by it, he always performs it, without murmuring or caviling; that he takes no unjust advantage, does not lie upon the catch to supplant anybody, and scorns, in short, to do an ill thing, though he might gain by it; that his word is as sacred as his bond; that he never grinds the face of the poor, but

pays for his work cheerfully and readily, and is content to let poor men live by him; that he scorns to make mistake pass for payment, or lie upon the catch to trepan his neighbour; in a word, that he is a fair, downright, honest man; God has blessed him, and everybody gives him a good word.

(*CET*, II. 86-87)

Defoe recognizes, of course, that this is the description of an ideal and that most of mankind must fall short of it. He frequently plays as well on the theme of the guilt of the dishonest and remorseful tradesman: "For I must always be allowed to say, that absolute necessity too often forces distressed tradesmen to do things which they are penitents for to the the very last hour of their lives, and which their very souls abhorred in the doing" (*CET*, II. 128). He also recommends that tradesmen whose fortunes mend should attempt to make restitution to those they have wronged as soon as they possibly can. Doing so does not fully repair the harm but does serve as a sort of salutary penance. Yet as we might expect of Defoe, there are other reasons besides mere love of morality which should induce tradesmen and merchants to be honest in their dealings: frankly, he says, it is simply good business, for

> two things principally raise credit in trade; and those are, —
> 1. INDUSTRY: 2. HONESTY.
>
> I have dealt upon the first; the last I have but few words to say to, because that head requires no comment, no explanations or enlargements; nothing can support credit, be it public or private, but honesty; a punctual dealing, a general probity in every transaction; he that once breaks through his honesty, violates his credit; once denominate a man a knave, and you need not forbid any man to trust him. (*CET*, I. 275)

Because tradesmen cannot operate without credit, they must maintain a reputation for honesty, without which they will lose their credit and thus their business.

Occasionally, however, Defoe promotes honesty and fair dealing not with the arguments of self-advancement but with generous urgings to good citizenship: "it would not be unjust only, but malicious, if a tradesman who is got into a channel of trade by his success, and gained an estate, should purposely render that channel impracticable to others" (*CET*, II. 90-91). His detailed advice is often similarly compassionate; he recommends

> 1. Not to delay paying a just debt, if able to discharge it, but to pay it without putting his creditor to the charge of suing for his own.

2. Not to give any man trouble, though for a just debt, where there is any probability of obtaining it without, nor till all reasonable and friendly methods are tried to avoid it.

3. When obliged by necessity to go to law for his right, to do it with civility, with tenderness, without exposing the debtor more than needs must, and without putting him to more than necessary charges. (*CET*, II. 119)

From such examples as these it is plain that Defoe does indeed often recommend ethical courses of action in his writings on trade. It may be argued, of course, that his general statements on business ethics and honesty are merely so much lip service to responsible behavior. Such a charge would be difficult to answer, for inasmuch as he was deeply enamored of trade and often sought to dignify and elevate it, his motive for putting up an ethical front is thus established. It would be impossible to deny that there is some deliberate glamorizing of the tradesman's ethical posture by Defoe, for one has only to read his characters of the "honest, open-hearted, generous, fair-dealing tradesman" or of the abject, remorseful, dishonest tradesman to be aware that he is constructing ideal cases which favor trade. Even in his frequent recommendations of clemency for debtors, a subject which affected him quite personally, there is an occasional hint that he is attempting to heighten commerce, as when he describes the "hateful picture" of the "querulous, litigious tradesman" as being "the contempt of his rich, and the aversion to his poorer neighbors, the scandal of his trade, and the terror of his customers" (*CET*, II. 118). The responsibilities Defoe mentions here are those to one's neighbors (presumably trading associates), to one's customers, and to one's *trade*. Yet despite his ever-present, almost unconscious desire to dignify the trading profession, no one familiar with Defoe's life, with his loathing of debtors' prison, his periods as a fugitive from his creditors, or his continued efforts to compound with them could doubt that his recommendations of decent treatment of debtors is less than straight from the heart. His intentions may not be important; surely they are unprovable. The fact remains that he does treat ethical matters frequently in his tracts on trade.

DEFOE'S SYSTEM OF RETRIBUTIVE VIRTUE

A previously unnoticed aspect of Defoe's writings on business ethics is his development of a system of moral-economic justice. This system consists of his concept of what might be called retributive virtue and his contention that unethical actions are crimes against trade. Defoe's notion of retributive virtue is an almost Darwinian application of the Puritan ethic: the just and prudent man attains wealth, while the unrighteous and imprudent man sinks into poverty. Moreover, he tends to identify moral with prudent behavior. Throughout his works he frequently mentions "the ancient families worn out by time and family misfortunes, and the estates possessed by a new race of tradesmen, grown up into families of gentry" (*CET*, I. 244). Probing into the causes of these "family misfortunes," Defoe notes "how many of these great and noble families have been impoverished by the luxurious way of living which they have taken up in these latter ages of the world; and how have the estates of the great families been swallowed up by the commonality and tradesmen" (*Review*, III. 37). Denham describes this state of affairs in his lines,

> While luxury, and wealth, like war and peace,
> Are each the other's ruin, and increase.[22]

Luxurious living, as Defoe defines it, is living beyond one's means, and we recall that he advanced the opinion in the *Review* that no credit should be extended for luxury goods. Living beyond one's means is not only economically foolish, however; it is morally wrong, a symptom of the deadly sin of pride: "it is the trade that has made the common people rich, as pride has made the gentry poor" (*Plan*, p. 60).

Accordingly, ancient families, as consumers of luxuries, suffer a social loss for their moral turpitude and economic folly, while tradesmen are rewarded by increase in station for diligent application to their tasks:

> How has trade, thus first encroached upon nobility and quality; and when it has first made gaps in your most illustrious successors, by creeping into their estates, has again supplied you with crowds of gentry, and not a few nobility, to patch up the ruin of ancient luxury, and make good the desolation, made by unwary prodigality? (*Review*, III. 38)

As we have seen, it is the user of luxury goods, not the supplier of them, who is the guilty party in Defoe's scheme of things. Just as he identifies consumption of luxuries with evil, he makes thrift a positive virtue:

> I might enlarge here upon the differing effects of luxury and frugality... as the frugal manufacturers, encouraged by their success, doubled their industry and good husbandry, they laid up money, and grew rich; and the luxurious and purse proud gentry, tickled with the with the happy increase of their revenues, and the rising value of their rents, grew vain, gay, luxurious and expensive: so the first increased daily, and the latter, with all their new

> increased and advanced revenues, yet grew poor and necessitous, till the former began to buy them out; and have so bought them out, that whereas in those days, the lands were all in the hands of the Barons... so that now the gentry are richer than the nobility, and the tradesmen are richer than them all. (*Plan*, pp. 37-38)

This is a rough code of justice, and Defoe underscores it with his statement that "the business of trade is to get money — and if I can get money by trade, with getting it fairly, I am to do it against anybody's interest or advantage" (*Review*, VIII. 38). The definition of "fairly" of course is not forthcoming.

The message, nevertheless, is clear. Defoe's idiom is that of the Puritan ethic, and it is largely that ethic which provides the moral underpinnings and justification of his system. The celebration of diligence and perseverance, the approval of the acquisition of wealth, and the disapproval of the luxurious disposition of that wealth all loom large in Defoe's thought. Diligence amasses wealth; imprudence dissipates it: these are statements not merely of cause and effect but of principle. They also constitute a very constructive ethic. To build, to create, to amass and acquire slowly through one's sustained efforts may be thought a noble ideal when one considers that these results are achieved in the service of one's fellows. But to acquire wealth rapidly and seemingly effortlessly through the fluctuations of a financial market is a different matter entirely, for such lucre is unsanctified by the cleansing power of diligent industry. It may well have been feelings such as these, induced by an overdose of Puritan ethic, which motivated Defoe's hostility to financial markets in general and to the South-Sea venture in particular.

Such thinking certainly colored Defoe's imagery; one of his most frequently-repeated figures is that likening of an estate to a pond and trade to a spring:

> as estate's a pond, but trade's a spring: the first, if it keeps full, and the water wholesome, by the ordinary supplies and drains from the neighbouring grounds, it is well, and it is all that is expected, but the other is an inexhausted current, which not only fills the pond, and keeps it full, but is continually running over, and fills all the lower ponds and places about it. (*CET*, I. 245)

Because those involved in business played an active, and the nobility and gentry a passive role in England's economic progress, Defoe might feel that this system of retributive justice was soundly based. Throughout all of his writings on trade is an implicit acceptance of the economic changes within England as being beneficial to it nationally and to all its classes. Trade was dynamic, so he pronounced it good. Because the nobility and the established Church were on the decline they were to be condemned, not only because they were economically stagnant, but also because their stagnation was an actual impediment to making England the most powerful nation in the world. Defoe did not stop to consider that change has its destructive side as well and that the power of the nobility and the Church were in a relative decline precisely because of the growing power of the mercantile classes. If the workings of trade produced an absolute increase of the nobility's income from rents without any effort on the part of the nobility themselves, then he felt justified in not wasting any sentiment over the relative decline of the old order.

Another component of Defoe's system of moral-economic justice is his assertion that unethical business actions harm the entire business community. Just as his doctrine of retributive virtue is based on his belief that the consumer, not the seller of luxuries is the guilty party, Defoe's notion of unethical actions as crimes against trade is similarly rooted in his attitudes toward necessity. He starts by accepting the idea that "Necessity is the parent of crime" (here again we are uncomfortably reminded of Moll Flanders), and he says of tradesmen, "I allow it to be true, that they thrive, because they are fair dealers; but much more is it true that they are fair dealers because they thrive" (*Review*, VIII. 303, 301). He develops the concept that the vices of commerce are primarily crimes against trade itself and result in automatic punishment upon the trading community:

> Abuses in trade never increase so much, as when trade declines — men in business driven to innumerable shifts and subterfuges, to support their affairs, invade right, encroach upon justice, and dishonor themselves. Again they undermine one another, combine and confederate against one another; enter into engrossments, monopolies, combinations, etc. And, in short, they seem to make war upon trade itself. (*Review*, VIII. 301)

The engrosser of trade is the chief villain: "The overgrown tradesman is, in short, a trading tyrant, and he tyrannizes in a most unjust and unreasonable manner over all the tradesmen of his own class; nay, he tyrannizes over trade itself" (*CET*, II. 112-13); "by this practice he becomes an oppressor, nay, a plunderer, a mere trading dragoon, and destroys not the tradesman only, but trade itself" (*CET*, II. 86). Such a monopolist is in a position to destroy his competitors, to take unfair advantage of his employees and customers, to "grind down" his manufacturer-suppliers, and to deny a promising future to his apprentices. The end result of such a course of action is to retard a particular branch of trade. There is another crime against England's trade which Defoe the mercantilist views as a threat to the national economy, and he speaks of it in these terms:

> there are vices in trade which I would direct the complete tradesman to avoid, and which tend indeed to destroy our trade, to wound it in the most tender parts, and to expose it, in the end, to a total decay, if not to death and destruction.   (*CET*, II. 244)

The "vices" here to which he refers is the importation of luxury goods ("the tawdry and sorry trifles of strangers"); such imports are, in the protectionist's view, a real threat to the security of the national economy and of trade itself.

This doctrine of unethical actions as crimes against the business community parallels that concerning overconsumption of luxuries by the landed classes: ancient families who foolishly overindulge lose their patrimonies; hard-pressed or overgrown tradesmen who encroach upon their fellows lower themselves and the entire trading community. Together these two concepts form a vaguely defined but rough-and-tumble code of moral-economic justice. The vices involved may be crimes against morality, but the punishment inflicted is economic in nature.

Defoe's writings on business ethics are scattered, often vague, occasionally contradictory attempts to deal with an enormously complex subject. Much of his contradiction and confusion seems to stem from his awareness of many of the complications involved. For the most part, later critics of his business ethics appear to have been blissfully unaware of the tangle of contrary ethical impulses which often may be operating on a single business decision; Defoe presents an easy target for their moral aspersions. He was not a perfect man, nor is he always a logical reasoner, but he does seem to have earnestly struggled toward a solution to the ethical dilemmas he deals with, and he did at least reach conclusions which are amenable to his own beliefs on necessity, mercantilism, and the Puritan ethic.

CHAPTER V

Defoe's Reputation

When Defoe died in 1731, aged, ill, solitary, and harassed by creditors, he had produced not only a vast number of writings but had also provoked a sizable number of printed attacks by political and personal antagonists. These attacks, along with some slightly more amiable literary criticism, provide perhaps the best available index of the way Defoe was perceived in his own day and of the particular aspects of his career and writings which were seen as being the most controversial. An analysis of such opinions should, therefore, yield information not only on Defoe's strengths and weaknesses but also on the generally accepted social and literary standards of the early eighteenth century.

Defoe's direct influence on commercial thought seems to have been limited largely to his own lifetime. His major commercial works, the *Review*, *Tour*, *Essay upon Projects*, *Plan of the English Commerce*, and *Complete English Tradesman*, are all available to twentieth-century readers, but they have become the province of scholars rather than of business executives. Today, moreover, economic historians are much less interested in his opinions than in his factual observations. Except for short selections or quotations, his commercial tracts were rarely reprinted in the nineteenth century and cannot be thought to have had any great impact upon the rapidly-changing British economy of that period. Although his commercial works were reprinted in the eighteenth century, all but the *Tour* were reissued only three or four times each, and none more than a decade after his own death. Whatever direct impact Defoe may be thought to have had is probably limited, therefore, to the first half of the eighteenth century. An investigation of contemporary opinions of Defoe might help discover the extent of his effectiveness as a commercial commentator.

Defoe's great claims for commerce are that it is a system pleasing to God's sight, that it is a bulwark of the nation, that it provides educational self-improvement and social advancement to those who practice it, and that it is an ethical undertaking. Yet he himself was attacked for his failure to exemplify each of these characteristics. Although he might describe business as pleasing to God, he was himself often described as "the most Unserene Daniel Foe, Clergy-Flogger in Ordinary to his Highness the Prince of Darkness,"[1] or as "a friend to hell and enemy to heaven."[2] Though he might tout business as being crucial to the safety of the nation, he himself was a public reprobate and a criminal. Though he might stress the educational value of being a merchant, on occasion he could admit, "I easily acknowledge myself blockhead enough to have lost the fluency of expression in the Latin, and so far trade has been a prejudice to me" (*Review*, II, 149), and John Gay could agree:

> the poor Review is quite exhausted, and grown so very contemptible, that though he has provoked all his brothers of the quill round, none of them will enter into a controversy with him. This fellow, who had excellent natural parts, but wanted a small foundation of learning, is a lively instance of those wits who, as an ingenious author says, "will endure but one skimming."[3]

Though Defoe might emphasize the economic benefits of practicing trade, he himself had little to show for his efforts. Though he might attempt to stress the ethical nature of commerce, an outraged Charles Lamb could later interpret *The Complete English Tradesman* as a catalogue of "the pompous detail, the studied address of every mean art, every sneaking address, every trick and subterfuge, short of larceny, that is necessary in the tradesman's occupation."[4]

Defoe was thus vulnerable to attack from a number of directions. As a controversialist, it is hardly surprising that he was abused in print, but unlike many controversialists, he did not attract a coterie of defenders; such defenses as one finds — particularly those which see in Defoe "eminency of gifts, humility of spirit, elegancy of style, solidity of matter, height of fancy, depth of judgment, clearness of apprehension, strength of reason, and ardent zeal for truth,"[5] — one is not surprised to discover to have been attributed to Defoe himself.

Besides being a controversialist, Defoe was unquestionably one of the leading apologists of his time for commerce, industry, and the middle classes. He was so recognized in his own day because of the forcefulness and the extent of his non-fictional writings on these subjects; he is so remembered today largely because his fiction has lifted him above the obscurity which covers many of his competitors and antagonists. Despite his technical competence as a commercial commentator, however, one might ask whether he was perhaps an unfortunate spokesman for business. While becoming ever more clearly identified as a proponent of business, he also became progressively more entangled in political controversy and increasingly more embarrassed by his personal affairs. Personal attacks on the champion of business, inspired by whatever reasons, might perhaps have affected his commercial cause.

DEFOE'S TENDENCY TO WEAKEN HIS OWN POSITION

Defoe's rivals and antagonists seem to have missed his tendency to undercut subtly his own position. Despite his deliberate advocacy of the importance and dignity of business, he at times lets his imagery confound his purpose. Consider these examples from the *Review*, written less than six months apart:

> Not the variety of the climates, not the beauty of the heavenly bodies, not the influences of the elements in the productions of nature; not the harmony of the creation in general, or the wonderful operations of the parts in particular, afford a more profitable, instructing, and diverting observation, than the pleasing diversity of nature, from whence is derived the foundations of commerce, and the chain of happy causes and consequences, which has now, more than ever, embarked the whole world in a diligent application to TRADE. (February 5, 1713)

> Writing upon trade was the whore I really doted upon. (June 11, 1713)

Similarly, while he is usually at pains to illustrate the fitness of merchants to be considered gentlemen, he at times describes the wealthy tradesman as a poor "shadow of a gentleman" who still bears the demeanor of "the stock jobber, the 'Change Alley' broker, the projector" (*CEG*, pp. 258, 259); in the *Essay upon Projects* he first discourses on "house-breakers, highwaymen, clippers, coiners, etc." before describing "cunning" and "honest" projectors:

> Others being masters of more cunning than their neighbours, turn their thoughts to private methods of trick and cheat, a modern way of thieving, every jot as criminal, and in some degree worse than the other, by which honest men are gulled with fair pretenses to part from their money, and then left to take their course with the author, who skulks behind the curtain of a protection, or in the Mint or Friars, and bids defiance as well to honesty as to the law.
>
> Others yet urged by the same necessity, turn their thoughts to honest invention, founded upon the platform of ingenuity and integrity.
>
> (*Essay*, p. 11)

The instances of these contrasts are notable because of the peculiar forcefulness and quotability of their negative side. Their relatively infrequent occurrence, however, especially when compared to the mass of material Defoe wrote on commerce, apparently prevented Defoe's antagonists from using them as a basis for assault.

Analogous to his tendency to undercut his own position is the surprising animus he showed against Sir Richard Steele in the successful Tory plot to remove Steele, a chief Whig spokesman, from the House of Commons. Defoe, unsolicited, sent the Tory leadership selections from Steele's writings which Defoe considered seditious. Not only was Steele one of the few contemporary publicists who had given Defoe no motivation for such an attack; he also held views strikingly similar to those of Defoe on the value of business in society: "the courtier, the trader, and the scholar, should all have an equal pretension to the denomination of an gentleman."[6] Defoe's motivation in this affair may not be fully discoverable, but it is undoubtedly linked to his jealousy of a more successful rival journalist. Such an act on Defoe's part indicates that his emotions could occasionally get the better of his ideological attachment to business as a cause.

Interestingly enough, despite innumerable journalistic attacks upon Defoe, his attachment to business apparently was not instrumental in arousing the animus of his antagonists. As was stressed earlier, business was a largely non-controversial, even a politically bi-partisan matter in Defoe's lifetime, although certain snobbish attitudes toward traders survived. Accordingly, Defoe was attacked for having been a tradesman but not for being a champion of trade. More surprisingly, even certain controversial aspects of his praise of commerce seem to have been overlooked by his antagonists, most notably his unabashed exaltation of city, particularly London, life. There were vigorous traditions among both the poets and the economic writers of the day which denounced the filth, the crowding, and the smoke and smells of the city. One is left with the unsettling feeling that his antagonists did not bother to read Defoe's commercial works but merely copied each others' style in their assaults. The attacks directed against him fall into two broad categories, those which ridiculed his writings and those which impugned his character.

DEFOE THE "SCRIBBLER"

The Augustan period in England, despite its contumelious journalism, paid a great deal of respect to refinement and polish in literature. Defoe suffered the derision of rival journalists for being an unpolished scribbler; nor did the appearance of *Robinson Crusoe* materially alter this view of him, because the book was a success primarily with the less cultivated classes. Disparagement of Defoe's literary talents became commonplace, and as Michael Shinagel suggests, "apparently he was fair game for the sneers of any aspirant to a groat's worth of wit, as well as for the real wits of the age."[7] Swift referred to Defoe and John Tutchin together as "two stupid illiterate scribblers, both of them fanatics by profession";[8] Martinus Scriblerus' *Peri Bathous* ironically praises Defoe for his "profundity." Alexander Pope, however, while he left no written record of any compliment to Defoe, was quoted by John Spence as saying, "The first part of *Robinson Crusoe* is very good. — DeFoe wrote a vast many things, and none bad, though none excellent, except this. There is something good in all he has written."[9] That Pope, whose polished verse is at the farthest remove from Defoe's hurried prose, should nevertheless recognize Defoe's literary skill, speaks well of his critical powers, but the fact that he chose not to commit such praise to writing indicates once again Defoe's lack of standing in refined circles. Lesser wits indeed made great sport of Defoe the "scribbler":

> Let banter cease, and poetasters yield,
> Since famed DeFoe is master of the field.[10]

A more lively variation on this theme seems to have been provoked by the extraordinary popularity of Defoe's "True-Born Englishman":

> First view him in his *True-Born English Farce*,
> With all his ten editions as his *Arse*,
> That heap of rhymes and dunghill of offense,
> Where all the guts are cast of impudence;
> A common laystall of his own disgrace,
> That shows him far less politic than base.[11]

While attacks such as these were fairly usual occurrences, even more frequent were the rather regular disparagements of his ideas and character by his fellow journalists, particularly John Tutchin in the *Observator* and Charles Leslie in the *Rehearsal*. Defoe responded to these in kind, but their net result was to surround his name with that skepticism we accord controversialists. The repeated *ad hominem* scurrilities of the pamphleteers, however indecent or unfair, could hardly elevate his reputation: "I fancy you [Defoe] to be the spawn of both nations, got by a *Dutch Pot-Hero* upon an *English Fish-wife*; deriving the wit of your arguments from the first, and the delicacy of your language from the last."[12] Charles Gildon even attacked Defoe ostensibly for what is surely his least offensive project, *Robinson Crusoe*, ridiculing Defoe's writings as "scribbling," along with his pantile works, his shifts to evade his creditors, his duplicity in party writings, his experience in the pillory, and even his having added the prefix "De" to his surname.

Another of the charges leveled against Defoe as a writer by his contemporaries is that of being a liar. His pre-*Crusoe* literary reputation was often said to consist in "the little art he is truly a master of, of forging a story and imposing it on the world for truth,"[13] and there is no lack of offhand references to "that illiterate blockhead *Daniel deFoe*... lying in a bad cause."[14] Defoe's reputation as a liar continued into the nineteenth and twentieth centuries. William Minto termed him "perhaps the greatest liar that ever lived,"[15] and G. D. H. Cole maintains that "everyone knows him [Defoe] for one of the world's greatest liars."[16] Shinagel agrees that "Defoe was not above making... flattering claims for himself," such as his claim to be "'related to' blood of none other than Sir Walter Raleigh." Shinagel mildly comments that "the contention is outlandish, but understandable when we consider that, as Professor Moore notes, Defoe was a lifelong admirer of Sir Walter Raleigh."[17] The contention is certainly "outlandish," but it becomes "understandable" only after one has thoroughly accepted the contention that Defoe is indeed an inveterate liar.

Defoe's reputation as a writer was under attack both before and after the publication of *Robinson Crusoe*. Most of the attacks, other than those by rival economic publicists such as John Tutchin, seem to have been inspired not by his commercial writings but instead by his political works, and he apparently was not satirized for having championed the cause of business. Rival economic writers might choose to argue particular points with Defoe, but they were in no position to deride him for writing about business. Other antagonists chose to attack him not for having written on business but for having failed at it or for having gained an unsavory political reputation, biographical matters to which we now turn.

MOTIVES FOR CONTEMPORARY ATTACKS ON DEFOE

James Sutherland has called Defoe "one of the most frequently abused authors of his generation."[18] His attackers saw that his social standing presented a fine target for their abuse. Defoe, the son of a tallow-chandler, was of middle-class origins and also a Dissenter. This might not have been a socially fatal combination — Alexander Pope was a

Roman Catholic and the son of a merchant, and Matthew Prior was the nephew of a tavernkeeper — had he not become the vocal champion of both groups. Perhaps he would have fared better in America, where Dissenters and the merchant classes were not social underdogs but the establishment. Superficially, at least, his career resembles that of Benjamin Franklin, with his middle-class origins, his interest in journalism and politics, his written advice to the small tradesman, and his schemes for civic improvement.

But in England, Defoe's social status was a real handicap. Although he was always at great pains to declare that he was a wholesale, not a retail, merchant, his enemies took great delight in terming him a "hosier": "Daniel Foe, at that time a hosier in Freeman's Yard, Cornhill";[19] or "and from a broken hosier, turned a scribe."[20] It was of little avail for Defoe to deny in the *Review* (II, 149-50) having been a hosier. John F. Ross maintains that "Defoe is confident of the value and growing power of his trading class; but he must protestingly accept its lack of social recognition."[21] As we have seen, however, it is only in the posthumous *Complete English Gentleman* that Defoe acquiesces to such a conclusion. In the *Tour*, the *Complete English Tradesman*, and his other commercial works, the striking feature of Defoe's thought is precisely that he does not make such an admission but continually equates economic well-being with good social standing, asserting that mere acquisition of a country house conveys both a title to the property and a claim to the social standing of the former owners as well.

Nevertheless, it is the "lack of social recognition" of the trading classes, not Defoe's recorded attitudes toward them, which represent the reality of Defoe's time. Boswell later quotes Dr. Johnson's praise of Defoe's works, "allowing a considerable share of merit to a man, who, bred a tradesman, had written so variously and so well."[22] The social reality of the period is also captured in a vignette in Johnson's "Life of Prior": Matthew Prior, the nephew of a tavern-keeper, became a fellow of St. John's College, Cambridge, and was known as an able diplomat, a charming companion of the great, a convivial wit, and a fine poet, yet Johnson records that the Duke of Shrewsbury, when he was to have joined Prior in negotiating the Peace of Utrecht, "refused to be associated with a man so meanly born."[23] Despite Steele's attempts in the *Tatler* and *Spectator* papers to make breeding, not birth, the test of a gentleman, despite Defoe's attempts to equate social with economic standing, and despite occasional indications that the social climate was indeed changing (Johnson's comment that "an English merchant is a new species of gentleman,"[24] for instance), there remained a good deal of social prejudice against the trading classes, particularly against small or retail tradesmen.

Compounding Defoe's problem with his reputation were his business failures, which, by reducing him to penury, not only spoiled his dreams of increasing his social status (rich merchants, after all, were able to advance in the world in spite of the social prejudice they might encounter), but in retrospect, rendered him ludicrous. The man who was singing the praises of trade and who had written that "the business of trade is to get money" (*Review*, VIII, 38) was himself a bankrupt, a debtor, a fugitive imprisoned for debt, who spent much of his life fleeing his creditors, and who died in hiding. The notable literary success of *Robinson Crusoe* contrasted with the dismal economic failure of its author would in almost any other case be material for romance. But for Defoe, a spokesman of business and an actual trader in an age in which Pope was proving that an author could live well by the pen, failure to realize an income from his writing is evidence merely of a lack of business acumen. Harry Ransom notes, "of the great publishing successes in this field [the novel], *Robinson Crusoe* was first; largely on Defoe's writing William Taylor built a fortune of £50,000. Defoe, however, was not rewarded proportionately."[25]

Prudence, that virtue which Adam Smith was to call the requisite of economic man, was the chief quality Defoe lacked. Inattention to his business affairs while pursuing his literary and political interests, as well as an unchecked speculative bent, seem to have been his downfall. His immoderate act of running off to join Monmouth's ill-fated Rebellion, his intemperate composition of *The Shortest Way with the Dissenters*, which led to his being imprisoned for sedition and pilloried while his brick and pantile factory went to ruin, and his overextending himself while heavily in debt to buy seventy civet-cats for perfume manufacture —such activities provoked a contemporary pamphleteer to make this derisive reference to Defoe's commercial failures: "He has run through the three degrees of comparison, *Pos.* as a *Hosier*; *Compar.* as a civet-cat merchant; and *Super.* as a *Pantile* Merchant."[26] In the affair of the civet-cats, he apparently defrauded his mother-in-law of almost £600, a matter which, as it moved through the courts, could hardly have enhanced Defoe's reputation as a man of probity.

Of all the forces working against his reputation, however, Defoe's political troubles had the greatest effect. Although he did not receive the pelting with rotten fruit and dung that was the London crowd's usual reaction to the sight of someone in the pillory — indeed, he received something of popular acclaim in the three days he was exposed there — "Defoe's reputation was, in a sense, damaged beyond repair with the more thoughtful public."[27] Shinagel agrees, maintaining that Defoe's "enemies were never to let him forget he was a pilloried man of letters, a disgrace he had to bear like a stigma."[28] Satiric references to Defoe in the pillory became legion, whether in the form of Dr. Thomas Dibbens' Latin verses on the subject, Swift's parenthetical reference to "the fellow that was pilloried I forget his name,"[29] or Pope's couplet in the *Dunciad*:

> Earless on high, stood unabashed DeFoe,
> And Tutchin flagrant from the scourge below.[30]

Defoe gathered many of the observations he later made in the *Tour* while touring the country as a secret agent for the chief Tory minister, Robert Harley, Earl of Oxford, during some of the periods when the wrath of his creditors made it convenient for him to be out of London. When he was able to return to London, he worked as a perpetual double agent, changing sides with administrations, writing for both Tory and Whig journals, and scuttling the position of first one side and then the other. His efforts were noticed and commented upon. In a poem entitled "A Dialogue between Louis le Petite and Harlequin le Grand," Defoe is described as Harlequin le Grand's (Harley's) "little Scribbler, Spy, Champion, Closet-Counsellor, and Poet, D----l D'F--e," and he is represented as saying to Harley"

> How oft have I imposed upon the crowd,
> And whispered T-----n, 'till 'twas talked aloud,
> That you your lucky cards might better play.
> And win the doubtful game *The Shortest Way*?[31]

Another pamphlet, entitled *Judas discover'd and caught at last*, cries out:

> Of all the writers that have prostituted their pens, either to encourage faction, oblige a party, or for their own mercenary ends; the person [Defoe] here mentioned is the vilest and an animal who shifts his shape oftener than Proteus and goes backwards and forwards like *a hunted hare*; a thorough-paced, true-bred hypocrite....[32]

An irate Scottish preacher quoted these objections to Defoe:

> he is a man of great rashness and impudence, a mean mercenarie prostitute, a state montebank, an hackney tool, a scandalous pen, a foul-mouthed mongrel, an author who writes for bread and lives by defamation.[33]

Defoe's political troubles, his social standing, and his business failures all drew the fire of his antagonists. Attacks in these areas, together with his reputation as a scribbler and a liar, must have hampered the embattled Defoe as a spokesman for any cause, despite the absence of overt attacks upon him as a proponent of business. At the least, such attacks apparently dictated much of his need for anonymity.

THE IRONY OF DEFOE AS A CHAMPION OF COMMERCE

Because Defoe was as unlikely a defender of the worth of business activity as John Wilkes was a champion of liberty, it is tempting to compare their careers. He is occasionally likened to Arthur Young, the great eighteenth-century popularizer of improved agricultural techniques. But Defoe's situation is in several important ways quite different from theirs. In the first place, the analogy with Wilkes breaks down because Defoe was not enshrined as the popular hero of his commercial crusade. Although he received the adulation of the mob while he was exposed in the pillory, his cause on that occasion was not a commercial but a religious and political one. Furthermore, while Defoe was attacked from almost every conceivable angle — as a literary hack, a social reprobate, a religious heretic, a political turncoat, and a commercial failure — he seems to have been accorded little abuse on the score of having defended business. His praise of business, in fact, appears to have been one of the few non-controversial aspects of his harried life.

The analogy with Arthur Young also breaks down rather quickly. A major similarity between the two men is that they were both popularizers of practical causes in which they themselves were failures. If anything, Young was an even worse farmer than Defoe was a businessman. Young, however, was the popularizer of improved agricultural techniques to increase productivity and efficiency. While Defoe occasionally touched on the matter of efficiency, he was concerned chiefly with delivering great generalizations on the importance and dignity of business. He expended most of his effort not in suggesting new commercial methods but in pointing out the benefits society received from merchants and the social rewards that were in turn due to them.

Ultimately we must ask whether business required the services Defoe devoted in its behalf and whether it benefited from them. The answers to these questions are speculative at best, but it is difficult to imagine that the commercial community of Defoe's day did not reap some benefits from his writings. In outlining the nature of Defoe's contribution, however, let us take care not to claim for him more than his just due. We cannot claim Defoe as the first or the only partisan of business, for despite some lingering social prejudice toward traders when he first began to propagandize, a favorable intellectual climate toward business was already developing. Nor can we claim any overwhelming personal victory for Defoe as an apostle of commerce. Most of his works were published anonymously, and neither the businessmen of his own day nor those of any succeeding age have seen fit to recognize him in any memorable way.

The quality of Defoe's achievement as a business apologist is largely determined by the nature of business activity itself, which is such that it does not require great effusions of popular sentiment to cultivate its growth, unlike that of a political campaign such as that waged by Wilkes. On the contrary, business thrives best through the steady, ordered, day-to-day attention of its proprietors, facilitated by a favorable climate of opinion in the wider culture in which business operates. To these ends Defoe labored mightily. In works such as the *Complete English Tradesman* he proffered good advice toward the diligent and profitable operation of business. In all of his commercial works he repeatedly emphasized the importance of the merchant's and the tradesman's calling, their place in society, and their service to the nation. These works were addressed chiefly to businessmen, and their bulk alone suggests some measure of impact.

It may be argued that despite his prolific output, however, the very general nature of Defoe's praise of business serves to blunt its appeal. This argument is answered by the realization that the business practitioners' day, their very life, is overwhelmed with innumerable details of accounts to be audited, sales to be made, manufacturing processes to be set right, employees to be dealt with. What the business person requires is not a recitation of more details but a statement of purpose which makes attention to daily affairs fit into a larger and more meaningful scheme of things. This Defoe supplied, certainly more fully than any of his likeminded contemporaries, among either literary or economic writers. Defoe's repetitive generalized praise of businessmen and their calling undoubtedly supplied feelings of basic worth and self-confidence to regular readers of the *Review* and other of Defoe's commercial works.

The novels and the *Tour*, with their sympathetic view of the merchant and tradesman, did indeed reach a wider audience. A fairly subtle presentation of the goodwill and good breeding of merchants by a single author might be capable of producing no great impact upon the popular mind, but Defoe's efforts in this line, added to those of contemporary writers and dramatists such as Steele and Lillo and coupled with the actual social rise of such men as Sir Joshua Child, may well have contributed to a collective effect. It was Defoe's fate that his attempts to increase the appreciation of business and businessmen in society should be shared with other literary and economic writers and that his responsibility for the apparent success of the overall movement should be largely indistinguishable from that of the other popularizers of business. That the movement was successful during Defoe's lifetime may be seen from his own situation: he wrote a great deal on behalf of business and businessmen, and his reputation, while it suffered from almost all else he attempted, did not suffer from his praising commerce. While he failed in virtually all of his own commercial ventures, he may be said to have succeeded as a popularizer of business. If the world loved a paradox, it would take Defoe to its heart: he stands in the history of business as perhaps its worst example and best advocate.

The twentieth century has witnessed the revaluation of Defoe on a sound and balanced basis, a welcome turn of events after the tendencies of his nineteenth-century biographers either to wholly accept or wholly reject the despicable portrait of him by his eighteenth-century detractors. Twentieth-century scholars are now seriously studying Defoe's moral, philosophical, economic, and social thought and are engaged in a project of editing his voluminous works. Modern evaluations of Defoe emphasize his "modernity," his intellectual toughness, his pragmatic and democratic viewpoint. J. R. Moore has done much to stress Defoe's relevance to the twentieth century, labeling him a "Citizen of the Modern World." Similarly, Marjorie Nicolson maintains that "Defoe's was a different eighteenth century [from Addison's] and one much closer to our own"; defends Defoe's integrity ("the opinions of Mr. Review... are not those of a hireling. They are the firm convictions of Daniel Defoe"); and suggests that his "purpose was the improvement of life and society in England." In the *Review*, agrees A. W. Secord, Defoe "was bringing philosophy out of the study." Defoe, says James Sutherland, writes "the prose of democracy" which possesses "a toughness of physical and intellectual fibre": "One cannot reject Defoe without denying the very principle of life itself."[34] Similarly, one can ignore Defoe's commercial works only at the cost of willing oneself to remain ignorant of the most important body of thought dealing with the place of business in an emerging industrial society.

NOTE ON THE TEXTS

Page references to Defoe's major commercial works appear parenthetically in the text, and the works are identified by the following abbreviations:

CEG   *The Complete English Gentleman*, ed. Karl D. Bulbring (London, 1890).

CET   *The Complete English Tradesman, The Novels and Miscellaneous Works* (Oxford, 1841).

Essay   *Essays upon Several Projects, Works*, ed. William Hazlitt (London, 1843).

Plan   *A Plan of the English Commerce* (Oxford, 1927).

Review   *Defoe's Review*, ed. Arthur Wellesley Secord (New York, 1937).

Tour   *A Tour through the Whole Island of Great Britain*, ed. G. D. H. Cole (London, 1962).

NOTES

INTRODUCTION

[1] John Robert Moore, *Daniel Defoe, Citizen of the Modern World* (Chicago, 1958); Maximillian E. Novak, *Economics and the Fiction of Daniel Defoe* (Berkeley, 1962); and Michael Shinagel, *Daniel Defoe and Middle-Class Gentility* (Cambridge, 1968).

[2] Maurice Ashley, *England in the Seventeenth Century* (Baltimore, 1952), p. 244.

[3] G. D. H. Cole, Introduction to Defoe's *Tour*, I, xiii.

[4] Ian Watt, "Robinson Crusoe as a Myth," *Essays in Criticism*, I (1951), 106.

[5] A. D. McKillop, *English Literature from Dryden to Burns* (New York, 1948), p. 150.

[6] A. D. McKillop, *English Literature*, pp. 259-62; Bonamy Dobree, *English Literature in the Early Eighteenth Century* (Oxford, 1959), p. 12f.; Ian Watt, *The Rise of the Novel* (Berkeley, 1957), chs. I and II.

[7] Bonamy Dobree, "The Theme of Patriotism in Early Eighteenth Century Poetry," *Proceedings of the British Academy*, XXV (1949), 63.

[8] R. D. Havens, "Primitivism and the Idea of Progress in Thomson," *Studies in Philology*, XXIX (1932), 41-52. Patricia Meyer Spacks, *The Varied God* (Berkeley, 1959), *passim*.

[9] Spacks' contention is that Thomson's best poetry in *The Seasons* tends to be in passages which describe a man-in-nature theme, a conception which is considerably more subtle than the notion of cultural primitivism, yet closely akin to it. Thomson, *Liberty*, ll. 437-38, Robertson ed., pp. 369-70. Compare Thomson's lines with those of Grainger: "thou [Commerce] does throw, / O'er far-divided Nature's realms, a chain / to bind in sweet society mankind." *Sugar Cane*, IV, ll. 350-52, *The Works of the English Poets*, ed. Alexander Chalmers (London, 1810), XIV, 507.

[10] George Sherburn, *The Restoration and Eighteenth Century* in *A Literary History of England*, ed. A. C. Baugh (New York, 1948), p. 830.

[11] A. D. McKillop, *James Thomson: The Castle of Indolence and Other Poems* (Lawrence, Kansas, 1961), p. 1.

[12] Edmund Burke, *First Letter on a Regicide Peace*, Works (London, 1803), VII, 145.

[13] George Rude, *Wilkes and Liberty* (Oxford, 1962), pp. 15-16.

[14] Charles Churchill, *Night*, ll. 239-40, *Poetical Works* (London, 1804), I. 110.

[15] James Beattie, "On the Report of a Monument," ll. 97-98, Chalmers, ed., *Works*, XVIII, 552.

[16] C. A. Moore, "Whig Panegyric Verse," *PMLA*, XLI (1926), 398-99.

[17] Swift, *Examiner* 21 (28 December 1710), *Prose Works*, ed. Herbert Davis (Oxford, 1957), III, 48.

[18] Burke, *Reflections on the Revolution in France*, Works (London, 1899), III, 359.

[19] Chesterfield, Letter LCVII (14 January 1751), *Letters to His Son* (Edinburgh, 1775), III, 119.

[20] Diana Spearman, *The Novel and Society* (London, 1966), p. 27.

CHAPTER I
DEFOE'S ECONOMIC ENVIRONMENT

[1] P. M. Deane and W. A. Cole, *British Economic Growth 1688-1959* (Cambridge, 1962), p. 40; W. Cunningham, *The Growth of English Industry and Commerce* (Cambridge, 1892), pp. 362ff.; J. L. and Barbara Hammond, *The Rise of Modern Industry* (New York, 1926), p. 21ff.; D. C. Coleman, "Industrial Growth and Industrial Revolutions," *Economica*, new series, XXIII (1956), 122.

[2] For this and the discussion which follows, I am indebted to a number of economic historians chief among whom are T. S. Ashton, *An Economic History of England* (London, 1955); W. S. Reid, *Economic History of Great Britian* (New

York, 1954); M. Briggs and P. Jordan, *Economic History of England* (London, 1962); and Deane and Cole, *British Economic Growth*.

3 Helpful on the South Sea Company are John Carswell, *The South Sea Bubble* (London, 1960); Lewis Melville, *The South Sea Bubble* (London, 1921); and Virginia Cowles, *The Great Swindle* (London, 1960).

4 Gregory King, "Natural and Political Observations," *Two Tracts*, ed. George E. Barnett (Baltimore, 1936), p. 18; F. C. Dietz, *An Economic History of England* (New York, 1942), p. 278.

5 *The Cambridge Economic History of Europe*, ed. H. J. Habakkuk and M. Postan, VI (1965), 6.

6 Helpful discussions of canonism are found in James Bonar, *Philosophy and Political Economy* (London, 1927); Harvey W. Peck, *Economic Thought and its Institutional Background* (New York, 1935); Raymond de Roover, "Ancient and Medieval Thought," *International Encyclopedia of the Social Sciences* (New York, 1968), IV, 430-35; and Benjamin N. Nelson, *The Idea of Usury* (Princeton, 1949).

7 Henry Robinson, *Briefe Considerations Concerning the Advancement of Trade and Navigation* (London, 1649), p. 2. Particularly enlighting on mercantilism are E. F. Heckscher, *Mercantilism* (London, 1934); Lewis H. Haney, *History of Economic Thought* (New York, 1949); Jacob Viner, *Studies in the Theory of International Trade* (New York, 1937) and "Mercantilism," *International Encyclopedia of the Social Sciences* (New York, 1968), IV, 435-42.

8 Viner, *Studies*, pp. 15ff.

9 N[icholas] B[arbon], M.D., *A Discourse on Trade* (London, 1690), p. 36.

10 William Lee, *Daniel Defoe* (London, 1869), I, 214-20. J. R. Moore, *Daniel Defoe: Citizen of the Modern World* (Chicago, 1958), p. 317.

11 Maximillian E. Novak, *Economics and the Fiction of Daniel Defoe* (Berkeley, 1962).

12 Novak, p. 17.

13 H. R. Trevor-Roper, *Religion, the Reformation, and Social Change* (London, 1967), p. 4. Chief among the participants in this controversy are Max Weber, *The Protestant Ethic and the Spirit of Capitalism* (London, 1930); W. Cunningham, *Christianity and Economic Science* (London, 1914); R. H. Tawney, *Religion and the Rise of Capitalism* (New York, 1926); Ernst Troeltsch, *The Social Teaching of the Christian Churches* (New York, 1931); S. A. Burrell, *The Role of Religion in Modern European History* (London, 1964). Robert W. Green, *Protestantism and Capitalism: The Weber Thesis and its Critics* (Boston, 1959) is a useful survey of the controversy before Trevor-Roper.

14 Tawney, p. 251.

15 Trevor-Roper, pp. 25, 27.

16 Important discussions of progress are found in J. B. Bury, *The Idea of Progress* (New York, 1955); R. F. Jones, *Ancients and Moderns* (St. Louis, 1936); J. A. Mazzeo, *Renaissance and Revolution* (New York, 1967).

[17] "The notion of gradual, continued progress, with no discernable limit, in a more or less linear ascent from an inferior condition, was unknown to mankind before the seventeenth century" (Mazzeo, p. 275).

[18] Thomas Sprat, *History of the Royal Society*, ed. J. I. Cope and H. W. Jones (St. Louis, 1958), p. 352.

[19] Thomas Baston, *Thoughts on Trade* (London, 1716), pp. 29-30.

[20] H. R. Fox Bourne, *English Merchants* (London, 1886), pp. 220-46. Sir Josiah Child and Sir Dudley North were not only immensely wealthy merchants but also prolific writers on trade, and although they made their fortunes in a period of predominantly mercantilist thought, their writings are often viewed as precursors of free-trade theories. For the discussion of eighteenth-century society, I am indebted to Dorothy Marshall, *English People in the Eighteenth Century* (London, 1956) and M. D. George, *London Life in the Eighteenth Century* (London, 1925).

[21] Gregory King, in Sir George Clark, *The Wealth of England from 1496 to 1760* (London, 1961), pp. 57-58.

[22] Sir Richard Steele, *Tatler* 207, August 3-5, 1710.

[23] Lewes Roberts, *The Treasure of Traffike* (London, 1641), p. 97.

[24] William Wood, *A Survey of Trade* (London, 1718), pp. 57-58.

[25] John Evelyn, *Navigation and Commerce* (London, 1674), pp. 11-12.

[26] Sir Dudley North, *Discourses on Trade* (London, 1691), reprinted in *A Select Collection of Early English Tracts on Commerce* (London, 1856), p. 540.

[27] Sir John Hawkins, *The Life of Samuel Johnson, L.L.D.*, ed. Bertram H. Davis, (New York, 1961), p. 113.

CHAPTER II
DEFOE'S PRAISE OF COMMERCE

[1] Defoe, *The Fortunate Mistress*, ed. G. A. Aitken (London, 1895), I, 193. Samuel L. Macey, *Money and the Novel* (Victoria, 1983), p. 166.

[2] Maximillian E. Novak, *Economics and the Fiction of Daniel Defoe* (Berkeley, 1962), pp. 33ff.

[3] While Downie notes correctly that Defoe "eyed stock jobbing, speculation, and commercial adventure with a cool lack of sympathy," he maintains as well that Defoe "regarded many changes with scepticism, and was far from being the harbinger of the Industrial Revolution." Indeed, we should take pains to discriminate between Defoe's financial conservatism and his industrial progressivism; he almost uniformly praises new *manufacturing* technology. J. A. Downie, "Defoe, Imperialism, and the Travel Books Reconsidered," *The Yearbook of English Studies*, XIII (1983), 78.

[4] George Chalmers, *The Life of Daniel Defoe* (London, 1790), pp. 67-69.

[5] James Sutherland, *Defoe* (London, 1937), p. 134. Macey, p. 18. In describing journalistic discussion of such economic issues as stocks, credit, and the Bank of England, Paula Backscheider contends that "no writer was more creative

in [explaining and debating these concepts] than Daniel Defoe." "Defoe's Lady Credit," *Huntington Library Quarterly*, XLIV (1981), 89.

6 As Peter Earle notes, Defoe's commercial writings "do not appear to have much conscious theoretical background, other than a rather breathless optimism," *The World of Defoe* (London, 1976), p. 107. G. D. H. Cole, Introduction to *Tour*, I, xv-xvi.

7 Defoe refers here to revenue from customs and excises, but he also frequently states that an increased trade raises rents and therefore land taxes.

8 Sutherland, *Defoe*, p. 47. John McVeagh, "Defoe and the Romance of Trade," *Durham University Journal*, LXX (1978), 142.

9 *The Cambridge Economic History of Europe*, H. J. Habakkuk and M. Postan, VI (1965), 6.

10 Michael Shinagel, *Daniel Defoe and Middle-Class Gentility* (Cambridge, 1968), p. 209.

11 Macey, p. 65.

12 Shinagel, p. 222.

13 See Shinagel, pp. 216-17.

CHAPTER III
DEFOE'S *TOUR* AS A PAEAN OF BUSINESS

1 Godfrey Davies, "Daniel Defoe's *A Tour Thro' The Whole Island of Great Britian*," *Modern Philology*, XIVIII (1950), 21.

2 Michael Shinagel, *Daniel Defoe and Middle-Class Gentility* (Cambridge, 1968). Pat Rogers, "Defoe and Virgil: The Georgic Element in *A Tour thro' Great Britain*," *English Miscellany*, XXII (1971); "Defoe as Plagiarist: Camden's *Britannia* and *A Tour thro' the Whole Island of Great Britain*," *Philological Quarterly*, XLII (1973); "Defoe at Work: The Making of *A Tour thro' Great Britain*, Volume I," *Bulletin of the New York Public Library*, LXXVIII (1975); "The Guidebook as Epic: Reportage and Art in Defoe's *Tour*," *Eighteenth Century Encounters*, ed. Pat Rogers (Sussex, 1985); "Literary Art in Defoe's *Tour*: The Rhetoric of Growth and Decay," *Eighteenth-Century Studies*, VI (1972-73); "The Making of Defoe's *A Tour thro' Great Britain*, Volumes II and III," *Prose Studies*, III (1981); "Speaking within Compass: The Ground Covered in Two Works by Defoe," *Studies in the Literary Imagination*, XV (1982). Rogers, "Defoe at Work," 432.

3 George Martin Barringer, "Defoe's *A Tour Thro' the Whole Island of Great Britain*," *Thoth* (1968), 5.

4 Samuel L. Macey, *Money and the Novel* (Victoria, 1983), p. 62. Shinagel, p. 206.

5 Shinagel, p. 201. See also Jo Ann T. Hackos, "Defoe's *Tour* and the English Travel Narrative" (Unpublished doctoral dissertation, Indiana University, 1972) in which she maintains that Defoe's purpose is to acquaint middle-class readers, particularly tradesmen, with the nation.

6 Rogers, "Defoe and Virgil," *passim.*

7 See Jeffrey Hart, "Johnson's *A Journey to the Western Islands*: History as Art," *Essays in Criticism,* X (1960), 44-59; Donald J. Greene, "Johnsonian Critics," *EIC,* X (1960), 476-80; R. K. Kaul, "*A Journey to the Western Islands* Reconsidered," *EIC,* XIII (1963), 341-50; Arthur Sherbo, "Johnson's Intent in the *Journey to the Western Islands of Scotland*," *EIC,* XVI (1966), 382-97. In successive issues of *Studies in Burke and His Time,* XIII (1971-72), there appeared Patrick O'Flaherty's "Johnson in the Highlands: Philosopher Becalmed," 1986-2001; Arthur Sherbo's "Some Antimadversions on Patrick O'Flaherty's Journey to the Western Island of Scotland," 2119-27; and O'Flaherty's "A Response to Arthur Sherbo's "Some Antimadversions on My Journey to the Western Islands of Scotland," 2229-33. T. K. Meier, "Johnson on Scotland," *EIC,* XVIII (1968), 349-52, "Pattern in Johnson's *A Journey to the Western Islands*," *Studies in Scottish Literature,* V (1968), 185-93, and "Johnson in the Highlands," *Forum for Modern Language Studies,* XII (1976), 189-93.

8 See Rogers, "Speaking Within Compass," 107ff, in addition to "The Guidebook as Epic" and "Literary Art," *passim* for a discussion of literary devices in the *Tour,* along with Geoffrey M. Sill's answer to the latter in "Defoe's *Tour*: Literary Art or Moral Imperative?" *Eighteenth-Century Studies,* XI (1977). Jo Ann T. Hackos maintains, even more ambitiously, that Defoe artistically unifies the *Tour*: "through the structure of the *Tour* itself and in actual descriptions of gardens, Defoe uses the metaphor of the garden to focus upon a visual ordering of the English language." "The Metaphor of the Garden in Defoe's *A Tour thro' the Whole Island of Great Britain*," *Papers on Language and Literature,* XV (1979), 261.

9 Rogers, "The Making of... Volumes II and III," 110.

10 Alistair M. Duckworth, "'Whig' Landscapes in Defoe's *Tour*," *Philological Quarterly,* LXI (1982), 455.

11 Shinagel, p. 135.

12 Thomas Baskerville, *Journeys in England,* Portland Manuscript, II, 308.

13 T. Thomas, *Journeys in England,* Portland Manuscript, VI, 80.

14 Stuart Pigott, *William Stukeley: An Eighteenth-Century Antiquary* (Oxford, 1950), p. 35.

15 G. M. Trevelyan, *England Under Queen Anne* (London, 1930), p. 6.

16 Margaret Willy, *Three Woman Diarists* (London, 1964), pp. 13-14.

CHAPTER IV
DEFOE'S BUSINESS ETHICS

1 Samuel H. Miller, "The Tangle of Ethics," *Harvard Business Review,* XXXVIII (January-February, 1960), 59.

2 Thomas Fuller, "The Good Merchant," *A Cabinet of Characters,* ed. Gwendolen Murphy (London, 1925), pp. 64-66.

[3] Robert W. Austin, "Code of Conduct for Executives," *Harvard Business Review*, XXXIX (September-October, 1961).

[4] Paul Dottin, *The Life and Strange and Surprising Adventures of Daniel Defoe* (London, 1928), p. 258.

[5] Hans H. Andersen, "The Paradox of Trade and Morality in Defoe," *Modern Philology*, XXXIX (1941), 23-46. Denis Donoghue, "The Values of Moll Flanders," *Sewanee Review*, LXXI (1963), 287-303.

[6] Andersen, p. 39.

[7] Andersen, p. 46. Others have seen Defoe's thought as being more closely related to Mandeville's. See J. R. Moore, "Mandeville and Defoe," *Mandeville Studies: New Explorations in the Art and Thought of Dr. Bernard Mandeville (1670-1733)*, ed. Irwin Primer (The Hague, 1975), p. 119; Maximillian E. Novak, *Economics and the Fiction of Daniel Defoe* (Berkeley, 1962), pp. 137-38; Gilbert D. McEwen, "'A Turn of Thinking': Benjamin Franklin, Cotton Mather and Daniel Defoe on 'Doing Good,'" *The Dress of Words: Essays on Restoration and Eighteenth Century Literature in Honor of Richmond P. Bond*, ed. Robert B. White, Jr. (Lawrence, Kansas, 1978), 56f.; and Andrew Varney, "Mandeville as a Defoe Source," *Notes and Queries*, XXX (1983), 26-29.

[8] Donoghue, p. 287.

[9] Donoghue, p. 288.

[10] Eric Williams, *Capitalism and Slavery* (New York, 1961). Williams' view has been attacked by Roger T. Anstey in *"Capitalism and Slavery*: a Critique," *Economic History Review*, XXI (1968), 307-20. In addition, C. A. Moore has noted the general insensitivity of literary figures of the seventeenth and eighteenth centuries and of their reading public to the issue of slavery: "Whig Panegyric Verse," *PMLA*, XLI (1926), 389-96. For a comprehensive review of the attitudes exhibited toward slavery by Defoe and other literary figures of the period, see Richard Kaplan, *Daniel Defoe's Views on Slavery and Racial Prejudice* (Unpublished doctoral dissertation, New York University, 1970).

[11] *The Voyage of Don Manoel Gonzalez (Late Merchant) of the City of Lisbon on Portugal, to Great Britain*, in John Pinkerton, *A General Collection of the Best and Most Interesting Voyages and Travels in all Parts of the World* (London, 1808), II, 34. J. R. Moore attributes this posthumous voyage to Defoe.

[12] Donoghue, p. 289.

[13] Maximillian E. Novak, *Defoe and the Nature of Man* (Oxford, 1963), pp. 65-88. See also Robert James Merrett, *Daniel Defoe's Moral and Rhetorical Ideas* (Victoria, 1980), pp. 43-47, for a discussion of Defoe's attitudes toward necessity, along with discussions by G. A. Starr, *Defoe and Casuistry* (Princeton, 1971) pp. 64, 133, 175, and W. Austin Flanders, *Structures of Experience: History, Society, and Personal Life in the Eighteenth-Century British Novel* (Columbia, South Carolina, 1984), pp. 52-55.

[14] Donoghue, pp. 290-91.

[15] Donoghue, p. 291.

[16] Donoghue, p. 293.
[17] John Dryden, *The Hind and the Panther*, I, 11. 148-49, *Poems*, ed. James Kingsley (Oxford, 1958), II, 473-74. Ervin J. Gaines, *Merchant and Poet: A Study of Seventeenth Century Influence* (Unpublished doctoral dissertation, Columbia, 1953), pp. 196-98 and *passim* contains a wealth of similar uses of commercial imagery.
[18] Donoghue, p. 296.
[19] See for example William D. Guth and Renato Tagiuri, "Personal Values and Corporate Strategy," *Harvard Business Review*, XLIII (September-October, 1965), 123-132.
[20] Michael Shinagel, *Daniel Defoe and Middle-Class Gentility* (Cambridge, 1968), p. 134.
[21] Shinagel, p. 211. Geoffrey M. Sill also points out that on occasion in the *Tour*, Defoe is more severe upon commercial transgressions (smuggling) than upon highway robbery: "Defoe's Two Versions of the Outlaw," *English Studies*, LVIV (1983), 122-25.
[22] Sir John Denham, "Cooper's Hill," 11. 33-34, *The Works of the English Poets*, ed. Alexander Chalmers (London, 1810), VII, 235.

CHAPTER V
DEFOE'S REPUTATION

[1] *The Republican Bullies* (London, 1705), p. 8.
[2] *A Second Defense of the Scottish Vision* (1706), p. 3.
[3] John Gay, *The Present State of Wit* (London, 1711), p. 506.
[4] Charles Lamb, "The Good Clerk," *The Complete Works*, ed. R. H. Shepherd (London, 1875), p. 356.
[5] *A Reproof to Mr. Clark and a Brief Vindication of Mr. Defoe* (Edinburgh, 1710), pp. 7-8.
[6] Richard Steele, *Tatler* 207, August 3-5, 1710.
[7] Michael Shinagel, *Daniel Defoe and Middle-Class Gentility* (Cambridge, 1968), p. 90.
[8] Jonathan Swift, *The Examiner and Other Pieces Written in 1710-11*, ed. Herbert Davis (Oxford, 1957), p. 13.
[9] Joseph Spence, *Anecdotes, Observations, and Characters, of Books and Men*, ed. James M. Osborn (Oxford, 1966), I, 213.
[10] *An Equivalent for Defoe* (1706), p. 1.
[11] *The True-Born Hugonot* [sic], *or Daniel deFoe. A Satyr.* By a True-Born Englishman. (London, 1703), p. 12.
[12] *The Female Critick, or Letters in Drollery from Ladies to their humble Servants, with a Letter to the Author of a Satyr call'd "The True-Born Englishman"* (London, 1701), p. 118.

[13] *Read's Journal* (Quoted in DNB).
[14] *Have a Care what you say* (London, 1707), p. 1
[15] *Daniel Defoe* (New York, 1879), p. 165.
[16] Introduction to Defoe's *Tour*, I, xv.
[17] Shinagel, p. 47.
[18] James Sutherland, "Biographical Appendix" to Alexander Pope, *The Dunciad*, Twickenham Ed. (London, 1943), p. 437. Maximillian E. Novak takes a somewhat more optimistic view in *Realism, Myth, and History in Defoe's Fiction* (Lincoln, 1983), pp. ix-xii.
[19] John Oldmixon, *The Present State of the Parties in England* (1712), p. 319.
[20] *The True-Born Hugonot*, p. 10.
[21] John F. Ross, *Swift and Defoe* (Berkeley, 1941), p. 34.
[22] James Boswell, *The Life of Samuel Johnson*, ed. G. B. Hill and L. F. Powell (Oxford, 1934), III, 267-68.
[23] Samuel Johnson, "Life of Prior," *Lives of the English Poets*, ed. G. B. Hill (Oxford, 1905), II, 190.
[24] Boswell, *Life*, I, 491 n.
[25] Harry Ransom, "The Rewards of Authorship in the Eighteenth Century," *University of Texas Studies in English*, XVIII (1938), 55.
[26] *Observations on the Bankrupts' Bill* (London, 1706), p. 7.
[27] Ross, p. 7.
[28] Shinagel, p. 69.
[29] Jonathan Swift, *Prose Works*, ed. Temple Scott, IV (London, 1897), 8.
[30] Alexander Pope, *Dunciad*, II, 302.
[31] "A Dialogue between Louis le Petite and Harlequin le Grand" (London, 1709), pp. v, vii.
[32] *Judas discovered and caught at last* (London, 1713), p. 3.
[33] Quoted in Joseph Clark, *A Just Reprimand to Daniel Defoe* (Glasgow, 1710), p. 7.
[34] Marjorie Nicolson, "Introduction" to W. L. Payne, *The Best of Defoe's Review* (New York, 1951), p. xx. Arthur Wellesley Secord, *Review*, I, xv. Sutherland, *Defoe* (London, 1937), pp. 275-76.

DATE DUE

MAR 1 0 2008			

Northern Michigan University

3 1854 003 859 603

EZNO
PR3408 E25 M44 1987
Defoe and the defense of commerce

WITHDRAWN

PR 3408 .E25 M44 1987

Meier, Thomas Keith.

Defoe and the defense of commerce

**OLSON LIBRARY
NORTHERN MICHIGAN UNIVERSITY
MARQUETTE, MICHIGAN**